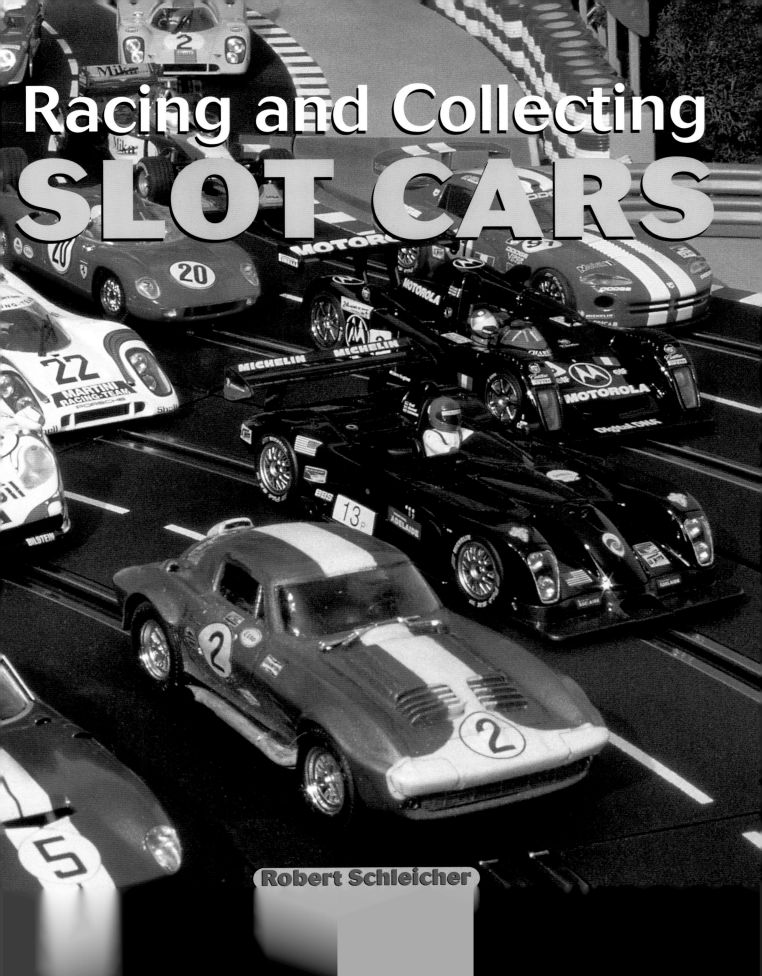

Racing and Collecting
SLOT CARS

Robert Schleicher

First published in 2001 by MBI, an imprint of MBI Publishing Company, 380 Jackson Street, Suite 200, St. Paul, MN 55101-3885 USA

The information in this book is true and complete to the best of our knowledge. All recommendations are made without any guarantee on the part of the author or Publisher, who also disclaim any liability incurred in connection with the use of this data or specific details.

This publication has been prepared solely by MBI Publishing Company and is not approved or licensed by any other entity. We recognize that some words, model names, and designations mentioned herein are the property of the trademark holder. We use them for identification purposes only. This is not an official publication.

MBI tites are also available at discounts in bulk quantity for industrial or sales-promotional use. For details write to Special Sales Manager at MBI Publishing Company, 380 Jackson Street, Suite 200, St. Paul, MN 55101-3885 USA

Library of Congress Cataloging-in-Publication Data
Schleicher, Robert H.
    Racing and collecting slot cars/ Robert Schleicher.
        p. cm.
    Includes index.
    ISBN-13: 978-0-7603-1024-3
    ISBN-10: 0-7603-1024-6 ·(pbk. : alk. paper)
    1. Slot cars—Collectors and collecting. I. Title.

TL237.2 .S35 2001
629.22'1—dc21   2001018740

On the front cover: You can build two-, four-, or six-lane home tracks with Carrera (shown), Scalextric, SCX, or Ninco track for 1/32-scale cars. The cars pictured here are Fly's Viper, Scalextric's Cadillac Northstar LMS, Fly's Panoz LMP Spyder, Carrera's 1998 Porsche GT1, a handmade Corvette Gran Sport with a Pattos body on a lengthened Ninco Cobra chassis, and a Pink-Kar 1963 Ferrari GTO.

On the frontispiece: Shown here are four 427 Cobra roadsters. The cars, from top to bottom are a 1/32 scale Ninco, Jason Boye's 1/58 scale on a AF/X chassis, Playing Mantis' Johnny Lightning HO body (a 260 on an AF/X chassis), and the Herpa non-motorized Cobra in true HO (1/87) scale.

On the title page: You can buy virtually every type of racing car you can dream of as a 1/32 scale slot car, and six of them can be races at the same time. The selection keeps growing and the model car manufacturers produce many new models each year. These are a couple of dozen of the hundreds of cars that were available when this book went into publication (and at least half of them are already out-of-production collector's items). The cars include American sports and GT cars, LeMans winning cars, Formula 1 Grand Prix cars, and classic sports and GT cars from the 1950s, 1960s, and 1970s.

On back cover top: The pit area on the Ascari track utilizes Scalextric pit buildings and figures. The Goodyear bridge and the grandstands in the background and the control tower are also Scalextric kits.

On back cover bottom: All of the cars in this book are designed to run as well as they look. Little maintenance, other than an occasional cleaning and some oil on the gears and bearings, is all that is needed to keep them runing. This is Carrera's 1967 427 Corvette.

Edited by Amy Glaser
Designed by Katie Sonmor
Cover by Dan Perry

Printed in China

CONTENTS

1

RACING MODEL CARS

A 427 Cobra, 1964 Cobra Daytona Coupe, Ferrari 330P4, and gold Ford GT40 Mark II round the Lowes Hairpin on Jason Boye's replica of the Monaco track. The cars are all HO-scale (1/58-scale) Boyes Models resin bodies on Mattel chassis and the track is Tomy-painted and detailed.

The car is skidding and sliding sideways around the turn, and is well beyond the limits of traction, but you slam on the throttle anyway. At that instant, the car's drift angle allows it to slingshot down the straight. When the car slows to a stop you realize it was only a model you were driving. Complete immersion in the action of that miniature car is one of the most exciting aspects of electric model car racing. Another is the fact that the car you are throwing about so wildly would be worth more than a million dollars in real life. It would cost an arm and a leg just to insure the real

thing, and almost as much to pay a mechanic to keep it running.

Model racing cars bring fantasies to life in a size that is affordable to buy and display, tune, maintain, and race.

Racing, for Real

For many years, I've enjoyed the hobby of racing model cars that were dead-accurate reproductions of the real cars. Some of you may have read my *Model Road Racing Handbook* published by Van Nostrand in 1967, and *Model Car Racing* published by Chilton in 1979. The years those books were published bracket the heyday of slot car racing. The cars available today and the newer plastic tracks make it possible to have realism and a driving challenge we could not have imagined in those days at prices about half of what they were during the heyday.

A joy of this hobby is that the cars are such accurate reproductions of the real racing cars that you will find yourself looking at the models just as you would look at a real car on a real race track. For instance, the size of your "visual image" of a 1/32-scale car is about the same size as your visual image of the real car when you view it from the distance of a trackside fence or grandstand. The realism begins with a near-perfect reproduction of the real car. When you actually start driving the car, the realism becomes so enveloping and perfect that you become immersed in a miniature world. Racing model cars is even more realistic than participating in or watching an actual car race on television or in person because you can see the whole car you are driving and not just the dashboard, windshield, and hood. You are controlling the car's smallest movements. Chapter 12 describes how you can powerslide, brake-slide, and induce understeer and oversteer. In chapter 5, you'll discover how to adjust the 1/32-scale equivalent of "aerodynamic downforce" that revolutionized race car design in the last 30 years.

Diecast Models and Slot Cars

The newest diecast models and kits are so realistic that you don't have to stretch your imagination to believe it is your dream car because it is–it's just reduced in size by 1/43 to 1/18 the size of the real vehicle. Look at one of the better diecast model cars from any angle and it's true to the original vehicle with all of the highlights on the curves, flowing shapes, and details, including hood latches and instrument faces.

Often, the only difference between a diecast model and an electric racing car is that the diecast model has a metal body while the

A Carrera BMW V12LMR and a Fly Panoz LMP Spyder roadster scream through a decreasing-radius ess bend on the Ascari track in Chapter 7.

electric racing car's is plastic. The racer, after all, has to perform as well as it looks.

You can admire one of the 1/18-scale static diecast model cars as a work of art, but when you watch 1/32-scale electric racing cars in action, the experience is on an even greater level than watching a real car race because *you* control the racing car.

Scale Model Car Racing

The most common sizes for diecast cars are 1/43-, 1/24-, and 1/18-scale–models that are, respectively, 1/43, 1/24, or 1/18 the size of the actual car. Electric racing cars are produced in 1/87, 1/64, 1/58, 1/32, or 1/24 scales. These numbers are fractions or proportions of full-size vehicles so the 1/87-scale cars are the smallest models, and the 1/18-scale cars are the largest.

The models in this book are limited to two sizes: "HO scale" and 1/32-scale. HO-scale models will operate on any brand of HO-scale track. Most of the HO-scale electric

Six Life-Like and Mattel NASCAR sedans thunder around the banked turn on Shawn Lee's HO-scale track. The track was routed from plastic sheet by Brad's Custom Tracks. Note the racing stripes of rubbed-off paint on the banking's wall.

The Paramount Ranch Track is a 1/32-scale reproduction of a real track, and measures 9 x 14 feet. It was routed from chipboard and took months to construct. You can assemble a track that's even more fun to race on in a couple of hours from Carrera, Scalextric, SCX, or Ninco.

racing car chassis are nearly the same size. The uniform size concept was developed because it was economically feasible to reduce an electric motor to fit the HO-scale chassis size. When HO-scale electric cars were first introduced in the 1960s, they were models of full-size American sedans that were intended for use on motorized roads as accessories for HO-scale trains. These relatively large sedans were 1/87-scale—the same size as the trains. The exact scale of HO racing car models varies depending on the prototype car that is being modeled. For example, the NASCAR cars are relatively large automobiles, and the HO model versions are 1/64 -scale. The Formula One cars and racing cars, including Porsches and Cobras, are somewhat smaller, so the HO models of these cars are 1/58 scale.

Most of the ready-built 1/32-scale cars are exactly 1/32 the size of the real car. Again, there is some adjustment so that smaller-sized cars reduced to exact 1/32 -scale can

compete with other 1/32-scale cars that would be somewhat larger. Some of the "classic" cars, including Ninco's Ferrari 166MM and Jaguar XK120, are about a scale foot (3/8 of an inch) wider than an exact 1/32-scale replica, but they are still realistic models.

Slot Cars or Electric Model Car Racing

I really do not like to refer to the models in this book as "slot cars" because they are not the same type of cars that many of us remember as slot cars from the 1970s. The cars in this book are mechanically identical to the slot cars of the 1970s, but the hobby has changed. The cars are still guided around the track by a slot. Similar to a model train, the cars receive 12 to 18 volts of DC (direct current) electrical

power from two metal strips that are flush with the surface of the race track. A pair of metal wipers or brushes beneath the car are in constant contact with the two metal strips. The electric power that is picked up through the strips is routed to an electric motor inside the car, which has a gear that drives a mating gear on the rear axle so the tires are what propel the car around the track. Since you control the amount of power that reaches the motor through a remote hand controller, you have a direct and almost instant effect on how fast the rear wheels are turning.

In the late 1970s, the hobby of slot car racing evolved to where the cars were modified or compromised into sleek wedge shapes vaguely similar to the real cars. The race tracks were expanded to the size of volleyball courts with eight lanes to accommodate the speeds of the slot cars. That segment of the hobby is still active and there are hundreds of slot car race tracks available on the internet. Most of the cars are 1/24 scale, but some of these shops do sell the better-detailed 1/32-scale and HO-scale cars that are shown in this book. There is also an active group of model car racing fans that are racing 1/24-, 1/32-, and HO-scale compromise model cars that have the high-speed chassis of the commercial raceway cars with bodies that are close to correct scale proportions. The compromise cars are seldom raced on the sectional plastic track. Their tracks are usually much larger and routed from sheet plastic or chipboard. It is usually possible to race a high-speed slot car on a plastic home track. Most of the scale-model electric racing cars you see in this book can be run on the commercial tracks, but it is also more fun to race the type of car that is matched to the track. If you are more interested in how your car performs than how it looks, you may want to investigate higher-speed racing.

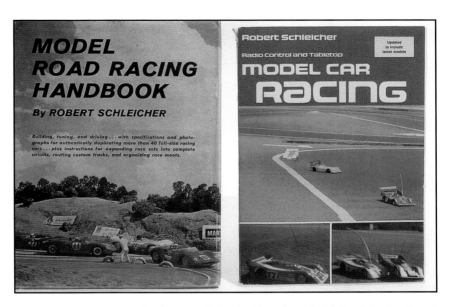

Books that are part of the history of the hobby: the *Model Road Racing Handbook* and *Model Car Racing*. The information supplied in this book, and the vastly superior cars and track make it much more fun and much less work to enjoy the hobby as it is today.

You can build the 1/32-scale track of your dreams on a portable, fold-up, ping-pong table. This Ascari 5 x9-foot Carrera track is described in chapter 7.

Time and Money

One of the joys of the new generation of model racing cars is that you do not have to build the car or the track. You can buy a ready-to-run replica of just about any popular prototype race car. If your favorite vehicle is rare enough that only a cast-resin or clear plastic body is available, the manufacturer of the body can sometimes supply a ready-to-run version, or you may locate a dealer who will build and paint the model for you. Also, the wide selection of plastic tracks makes it possible to build the most realistic and challenging two-, four-, six-, or eight-lane track without the need to use a router to cut the track from sheets of chipboard or plastic.

Electric model car racing is far less expensive today than it was in the 1960s or 1970s. You can buy a figure-8 HO scale set for $40, or a 1/32-scale set for $100. The majority of the HO-scale cars are less than $20, and most 1/32-scale cars range from $40 to $50. If you want custom-painted replicas, you may need to spend $100 or more for a car, or you can probably make it yourself from a clear plastic body, chassis, and some parts and decals for $50.

Places to Race

The cars and tracks in this book are all intended to be used in your own home. You can set up any HO scale or 1/32-scale plastic track on the floor and the track can be moved in "modules" of four or five sections so you do not need to completely disassemble a racing circuit to store it. If you assemble the

Some of the most famous race track corners can be re-created like this 1/32-scale "Corkscrew" assembled from Carrera track.

a standard ping pong table. The ping pong table can be folded up if you need to share the space with other members of the household, just as the 4 x 8 panel or door can be laid on its side against a wall to store the race track.

Usually, you can find all the drivers you want among your friends. If you're looking for more racers, express your desire to your local hobby dealer that carries model cars. You may also be able to locate people to race with in your area and other tracks through the internet's website listings. There's an index of websites in the back of this book. When you are searching the web, be aware that the majority of clubs and race tracks you'll find listed are huge eight-lane commercial-type tracks in both HO and 1/32 scale. To find tracks similar to those in this book, look for clubs that cater to Scalextric, Ninco, and Carrera 1/32-scale cars, and the Thunderjet types of HO cars.

track on the floor, the size is only limited by the size of the room. Many hobbyists find it more enjoyable to set up a race track on a tabletop than on the floor. Most tables are about 30 inches high, which is about right for a driving position. If you want a more realistic view, sit in a chair beside the track or just kneel down and watch.

The HO-scale electric racing cars are so small that you'd think you could race them in a relatively small space. In reality, the cars are so fast that it is difficult to enjoy them unless the track has a straight that is at least 5 feet long. Consider about 2-1/2 x 6-1/2 feet as the minimum space for an HO-scale electric model car track. That just happens to be the size of a standard door so you can use a door as a tabletop. It is possible to squeeze an enjoyable 1/32-scale track into 4 x 8 feet using the standard-size curves from the sets. However, I suggest that you consider 5 x 9 feet a minimum size table for 1/32-scale cars—the size of

Here are 19 examples of some of the most detailed 1/32-scale models and most are ready-to-race. The first six cars are models of American sports and GT cars, the second row are models of LeMans-winning cars, the third row are examples of current Formula One Grand Prix cars, and the last row are 1950s- and 1960s-era sports cars.

2 MODEL RACING CARS

If a car is popular in real life, there is probably a model available. These are Scalextric's "Beetle Cup" models of the New Beetle in 1/32 scale.

What you see on these pages are miniature reproductions of real cars. They are so incredibly realistic that it is really not fair to lump them under the general category of "models." These model cars are designed to be precise replicas of actual race cars, right down to the smallest sponsor decal. What makes them even more spectacularly realistic is that they actually move at speeds comparable to the real cars, and for some it is as challenging to control one of these models as it is a real car. The 1/32-scale cars are far better detailed and proportioned than the HO cars, but the HO cars are painted and lettered similar to the larger models. These model cars perform and look like the real ones, so why would you be surprised to discover that you can also control them like the real race cars?

The Mechanics of Electric Car Racing

The electric racing cars in this book are designed to run on a plastic track with a slot. A pair of metal strips is recessed into the track on either side of the slot. These metal strips provide the electrical power to the cars. The 1/32-scale cars have a "guide shoe" that pivots so it can maneuver the car around the track. Braided wire strips are positioned

from Ninco and Parma that also have the brake feature can be purchased, and wires can be added to the connector track sections as described in chapter 12 to add brakes to Scalextric, SCX, or Artin tracks. The brake essentially uses the motor itself as a generator, much like what happens in a real railroad's diesel locomotive when it is fitted with dynamic brakes. The brake feature makes it more fun to drive the cars because you have yet another control option, one that works especially well with the "point-and-shoot" driving technique described in chapter 12.

You Are the Driver

You have complete control over the speed of the car with the controller. In fact, there are accessory controllers that you can install (shown in chapter 12) that also provide brake action when you completely lift off on the throttle trigger or button. It would seem that the car would be guided around the track so no steering should be needed. The reality is somewhat

You can probably find a 1/32-scale model of your favorite race car, regardless of the make, model, or era. The first six cars are examples of modern LeMans cars, the second row includes classics from the 1950s and 1960s, and the third row contains modern Formula One Grand Prix cars.

on either side of this guide shoe to touch the metal strips on the track so the electrical power can reach the motor that is inside the model. HO cars are guided by a simple metal pin and have spring-loaded metal strips that touch the matching metal strips on the track. You control how much electrical power reaches the track car by pulling a trigger or pressing a button on a hand-held controller.

The Ninco and Carrera 1/32-scale sets and the Tomy, Life-Like, and Mattel HO sets all include controllers that have a built-in brake circuit. Accessory controllers

A pair of Carrera Porsche GT1 cars race around a Scalextric track made from the "Formula One" or "Le Mans 24 hr" set that has been expanded with an additional circle of track sections, but it still fits on a ping-pong table. A circle of Scalextric C8027 "outer" curves with C907 borders has been added. An additional C8044 and C186 straight track Borders and C8037 and C905 Borders are clipped in place so the cars have room to slide around the curves without hitting the fences. The buildings and people are also Scalextric.

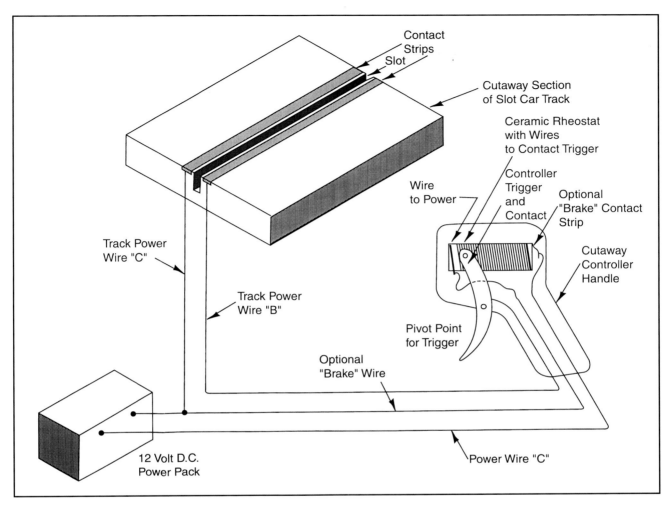

A wiring diagram of how the wiring and controller operate on a typical electric model car track. The third brake wire is only offered with Carrera and Ninco 1/32-scale sets and Life-Like, Tomy, and Mattel HO sets. You can add the brake feature to Scalextric, SCX, or Artin sets by soldering an additional wire to match a Ninco, Carrera, or Parma controller.

different because at racing speeds, you must learn to "steer" the car with the throttle as you would a racing car that was powering through a curve at the limits of tire adhesion. The slot will guide the car around the curve if you maintain a minimum amount of throttle pressure, but you are only driving the car around and not pushing it to racing speeds.

Models with Super-Power Traction

Nearly all of the HO scale and most 1/32-scale race cars have strong magnets mounted low on the chassis. These magnets grip the steel power rails on each side of the slot to help keep the car in the slot. The strongest magnets make it difficult to slide the car around the corners. The magnets in the 1/32-scale cars from Fly and MRRC are strong enough to hold the car to the track even if the track is vertical. The magnets in nearly all of the HO-scale cars are strong enough to hold the car to the track even if you turn the track upside down!

There's no agreement among model car racers about which magnet is the best: strong, medium, weak, or none at all. The weaker the magnet, the more difficult it is to keep the car in the slot, but you can enjoy the thrill of watching a car slide around a corner because the cars with strong traction magnets do not slide. Conversely, the stronger the magnet, the faster the car can go because it barely needs to slow down for the corners. I prefer the challenge of "steering" my model car around the corners with throttle control, so I remove the magnets from most of my cars. However, I do have some cars that have weak magnets, including the Scalextric Formula One McLaren and Jordan, that seem to produce an understeer effect (as described in chapter 12) that matches the performance of that particular car in real life.

Three Life-Like HO models of NASCAR Ford Taurus and a Mattel Pontiac Grand Prix thunder around a banked turn on a replica of the Darlington Raceway.

Some of the 1/32-scale cars from the 1960s have been reincarnated, including this ex-Monogram Ferrari GTO/LM and Chaparral. Both are now available from MRRC. The Chaparral is ready-to-run and the Ferrari is a plastic kit. The cars are racing on Steve Burkey's track made from Revell track sections still offered as the Riggen brand by R.E.H.

Valuable Collections

If you are in this hobby with the hope that you will make a profit on your investment, buy two of every car you like so you'll have one to "collect" and the other to race. The cars in this book are meant to be raced and not just collected. You will see some examples of model cars from the 1960s and 1970s that are only attainable through flea markets or eBay auctions. If it's the real car that interests you, rather than the collectibility of the model, you can re-create the real car without having to search for an out-of-production collectible. One of my goals in preparing this book was to provide the sources of bodies, chassis, and wheels so you can build a model of any real race car you wish as well as re-create replicas of any of the "collectible" model cars of the 1960s and 1970s.

The 1950s-era Indianapolis race cars once made by Strombecker are no longer available, but you can buy clear plastic Booth or Nostalgia-brand bodies, paint and decorate them with Pattos decals, then mount the bodies on an MRRC or EJ's chassis with exact-replica wheels and tires from Ninco's Cobra to produce replicas of 1960s-era Indy cars that are even more realistic than the "valuable" Strombecker cars.

Most often, you won't even need to build a "replica" of your favorite real car or slot car from the 1960s or 1970s because the real cars of those eras are so popular that the model manufacturers are re-creating them. In some cases–including the MRRC Ferraris, Cobra, and Chaparral–the bodies are molded from the same dies that produced the original models in the 1960s and 1970s.

Vintage and Modern Racing Cars

I can only provide a small sample of the hundreds of different race cars that you can build or buy for existing model products. Virtually any winning race car, from the 1940s to the present, is available in 1/32 scale. The selection is much more limited in HO scale, but the most popular cars are available. If

Strombecker offered their 1960s-era Watson Indy roadster with a set of decals to duplicate six actual race cars. These are the six painted and detailed (including drivers with the proper color helmets and driving suits) models by Russ Bundy. The wire wheels are Strombecker but there are now replicas of the proper Halibrand wheels from Ninco. The cars can be duplicated with Nostalgia or Booth clear plastic bodies, Pattos decals, MRRC 9802 brass chassis, or EJ's number 2A Inline Chassis with a NOS Strombecker open-style motor, and Halibrand-style wheels from Ninco's 427 Cobra.

you are interested in vintage car racing, you may discover that electric model cars are a far more exciting way to enjoy the hobby than just reading about the real thing. Static models, either diecast or built from kits, are more interesting to see first-hand than photographs or videos of the real cars. When you can see those miniature cars in motion, particularly if you are doing the driving, it is easy to forget they are models. You can re-create races with virtually every important car from the racing grid to see what it must have looked like to watch Phil Hill and Stirling Moss compete at the 1958 Targa Florio road race, or to be in control of Michael Schumacher's 1999 Ferrari while he dices with Mika Hakkinen in his McLaren. The model racing is real racing; the cars certainly look real, and *you* get to do the driving.

The original Airfix 1/32-scale models of the 1957 Maserati 250F and the 1957 Vanwall are now offered by MRRC as either complete kits or as bodies to be mounted on your choice of chassis.

Today's 1/32-scale ready-to-race "collector" cars are often standard models with special paint and lettering like these Porsche 908 Flunders that ran at LeMans in 1971 and 1973 from Fly. Both of these paint schemes are out of production, but others that are just as colorful are available now.

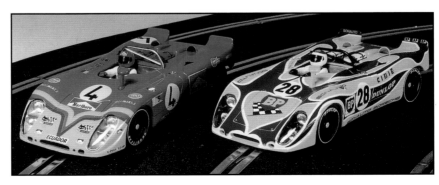

1/32 RACE CARS

Shown are six modern-era Formula One cars including a 1999 Ferrari from Pro-Slot, 1998 McLaren from Carrera, 1999 Stewart from Ninco, 1998 Sauber from Carrera, 1998 Jordan from Scalextric, and a 1998 Williams from Scalextric. There are about two dozen more Formula One cars available from these makers as well as SCX.

The new generation of electric racing cars, the models that were called "slot cars" in the 1960s and 1970s, is every bit as realistic as the best of the diecast cars. All of the electric cars are as realistic as the diecast models from "curb side." The electric cars do not have engine detail beneath the hood like the most expensive diecast models, although most have all the engine details that are visible through clear hood scoops or beneath the open tail. The newest electric racing cars often have interior details, just like the best diecast models, but these motorized models are meant to be raced and always include a driver figure.

Today's Scale Model Cars

Not every 1/32-scale car is as realistic as the next. There are different levels of realism and detail, even with the cars that are currently available. You can divide the appearance of 1/32-scale model cars into three categories: toys, stand-off scale slot cars, and realistic models. The toys would include most of the cars that were available in 1/32-scale sets in the 1960s and 1970s from Scalextric, VIP, Strombecker, Eldon, Cox, and some obscure makers. If the cars did look right, they were a slightly larger scale, somewhere between 1/29 and 1/30.

The new 1/32-scale electric model racing cars are extremely well detailed, and most have full driver figures and interiors as well as visible underbody detail like that on this trio of Fly cars: a replica of the Porsche 917 that won the 1000 Km at Monza in 1971, a replica of the Lola T70 MkIIIB that Mark Donohue ran at Sebring in 1969, and a replica of the Porsche 917 that won LeMans in 1971.

The term "stand-off scale" is used by flying model airplane hobbyists to describe models that look reasonably realistic from about 15 feet away. That describes the majority of the clear-bodied 1/24- and 1/32-scale cars with clear plastic bodies and brass chassis that are intended for racing on the eight-lane commercial tracks. Some consider that a different hobby and more of a sport because realism is often supplanted by a need for speed. This book is focused on the realistic racers and not the collector's toy or commercial slot cars.

Today there are considerable differences between models. Compare Artin's, Ninco's, and Scalextric's Mercedes CLK cars. All are 1/32 scale, but the Ninco car is more realistic than Scalextric's because it has finer details. The

Scalextric car is more realistic than the Artin car because the Artin car uses press-on decorations and Scalextric and Ninco have printed-on decorations. The quality of the newest scale model racers is even better; Scalextric's Cadillac Northstar LeMans racer and Fly's new Corvette C5-R have interior and chassis details and some etched-metal parts that make them as realistic as some of the 1/18-scale kit or diecast models. There were similar differences in detail in the 1970s. The Revell and Monogram cars were all very realistic. The early Cox cars, like the Ford GT40, were lovely, but later efforts were as toy-like as Eldon's. The techniques in chapter 5 can be used to upgrade some of these "toy" cars to match today's more-realistic electric model racing cars.

Racing Collectible Slot Cars

There are better uses for the limited space in this book than to fill it with a history of slot car racing. However, it might be helpful to put the hobby as it is now into perspective with what it was. It can be traced back to Lionel race car sets of the late 1800s and early 1900s. The hobby became popular in the late 1950s in England when firms like Scalextric and VIP produced 1/32-scale sets. Strombecker introduced 1/32 scale to the mass market in America in the early 1960s around the same time it was discovered that racing Aurora's HO-scale Model Motoring cars was more fun than just watching the cars drive around a model railroad layout. Slot car racing boomed in the 1960s when Revell, Monogram, and AMT produced 1/32-scale sets; Aurora, Tyco,

Six late-1990s LeMans racers: Ninco's 1999 BMW V12LMR LeMans winner, Fly's LeMans Panoz LMP Spyder roadster, Carrera's 1999 LeMans Audi R8R, Ninco's 1998 LeMans BMW C12LMR, Carrera's 1999 BMW V12LMR LeMans winner, and SCX's Ferrari 333SP.

and Faller produced HO sets; and just about every hobby manufacturer followed with sets and cars.

The above-mentioned models are products that form the nucleus of the collector side of model car racing. Collecting is a hobby unto itself and you can find the models on eBay and at flea markets. Unfortunately, very few collectors are willing to risk the collector value of their cars by racing them. Fortunately, the 1/32-scale cars and the HO cars that have been produced during the past five years or so are nearly all more realistic, quicker, more reliable, and handle better than any-

There are about a dozen exact replicas of previous LeMans winners including Carrera's 1999 BMW V12LMR LeMans winner (also made by Ninco), Carrera's 1998 Porsche GT1 (also made by Fly), SCX's 1991 Mazda 787B, Fly's 1971 Porsche 917, SCX's 1968 Ford GT40, and MRRC's 1964 Ferrari 250P.

Six early 1960s GT cars: a Revell Ferrari GTO (Pink-Kar makes one now), a Cobra Daytona Coupe built from a Top Slot kit on an MRRC Cobra chassis, a Corvette Grand Sport (made from a Pattos clear plastic body on a lengthened Ninco Cobra chassis), a Jaguar Lightweight Racing E-Type (from a Top-Slot body on an MRRC Chaparral chassis), an MRRC Cobra, and an MRRC Ferrari 275P.

Carrera produces exact replicas of the 1966 Chevrolet Stingray and the 1966 Ford GT350 Mustang. The Corvette has been upgraded with Halibrand racing wheels from Ninco's Cobra.

thing offered in the 1960s or 1970s. In fact, many of the best models from that period are being reproduced with modern paint and pad-printing. If you really want a model that's no longer produced, you can find a clear plastic or resin body and a chassis (as described in chapter 5) so you can re-create your favorite prototype race car from any era.

Sports and GT Car Racing Classes

In "classic" terms, a sports car is an open-cockpit roadster with a flimsy

Top
Artin offers a Mercedes CLK and a Porsche GT3 in their low-cost sets.

Left center
A variety of European sedan racers are available, including this Mitsubishi Lancer, Ninco's Alfa Romeo 155, and two Scalextric BMW 318 sedans. The silver BMW is a repainted model.

Below
Anni-Mini produces the Any-Slot models. The models have cast-resin bodies with etched-metal and injection-molded plastic details. They are designed to fit Ninco chassis. This is the Any-Slot Maserati Tipo 62 Long Tail Birdcage and 1955 Porsche 550RS Spyder. Both are replicas of cars that raced at LeMans.

top, and a coupe is usually a Grand Touring car, but it can also be a convertible if the top is luxurious enough. In the "Prototype" classes, cars are divided simply into roadsters and coupes. The roadster had no top whatsoever, although there were some years at LeMans where these racers had to be fitted with canvas "convertible tops." If you're willing to paint a cast-resin body or paint and mount a clear plastic or cast-resin body, you can probably find just about any real car you would want, from any era. I have limited this list to currently available specific examples that you can buy as 1/32-scale injection-molded plastic bodies or ready-to-run models. New models are added and older models are discontinued every month, so this is certainly not a complete listing, but when new models are introduced, it will give you some idea of what cars you can buy (or what cars you already have) to compete against the newest offerings.

Mass-Produced Production Sports Cars: Aston Martin DB5, Austin-Healey Sprite, Caterham 7, 427 Corvette, Cobra Roadster, Dodge Viper, Ferrari 166M, Ferrari F40, Jaguar XK120, Jaguar E-Type, Lotus 7, MGB, Porsche 356, Triumph TR4.

Limited-Production Sports Cars: C5-R Corvette, Callaway, Dodge Viper GTSR, Ferrari GTO, Ferrari 250LM, Mercedes CLK GT1, Porsche 911 Evo 1, Porsche 911 GT1, TVR Speed 12.

Prototype Sports Cars: Audi R8R, BMW C12LMR, BMW V12L-MR, Chaparral 2C, Ferrari Testa Rossa, Ferrari 275P, Ferrari 512S, Joest, Maserati A6GCS, Mercedes 300SLR, Panoz LMP Spyder, Porsche 908.

Grand Touring (GT) Cars: Ferrari F50, Ferrari 512M, Lister Storm, Lola T70 MkIIIB, McLaren F1, Panoz Esperante, Porsche 911 GT1, Porsche 911 Evo, Porsche 917, Ventura 600SLM.

Modern Formula One Cars: Arrows, Ferrari, Jordan, McLaren, Minardi, Sauber, Stewart.

Vintage Formula One Cars: 1966 BRM, 1967 Eagle, 1961 Cooper, 1961 Ferrari, 1957 Maserati, 1957 Vanwall.

NASCAR Sedans: Chevrolet Monte Carlo, Dodge Intrepid, Ford Taurus, Pontiac Grand Prix.

Indy, CART, and IRL Open-Wheel Cars: 1982 Brabham F1, 1992 Lola, 200 G-Force.

Sedans: Mini Minor, VW Beetle, VW New Beetle.

Trans Am Cars: 1968 Chevrolet Camaro, 1966 Ford Mustang, 1968 Pontiac Firebird.

Touring Cars: Alfa Romeo 155, Audi A4, BMW 318, Ford Focus, Ford Mondeo, Peugeot 205, Renault Laguna, Renault Megane, Vauxhall Vectra.

Rallye Cars: Jaguar XK120, Mini-Minor, Mitsubishi Lancer, Peugeot 306, Seat Cordoba, Seat Ibiza, Subaru Impreza, Toyota Corolla.

Pink-Kar offers a Ferrari GTO with a body almost identical to the Revell GTO of the 1970s.

Very few American IRL or CART open-wheeled cars are available. These three are currently available (left to right): Scalextric has produced this 1992 Lola CART car in a variety of paint schemes and MRRC is offering 1982 Brabham Formula One cars painted in Target (shown) and Pennzoil liveries. Etzel has a cast-resin body that is an excellent replica of the 2000 G-Force CART car to fit the Scalextric chassis.

Strombecker produced these early-1960s Watson roadsters in the 1970s and they are now collector items. You can find them on eBay or at flea markets. Russ Bundy restored, painted, and decaled these cars to be an exact match for Eddie Sach's and A. J. Foyt's cars. You can also build your own from a Pattos or Booth clear plastic body with Pattos decals and an MRRC Clubman chassis. Any "rare" slot car can virtually be re-created by building your own.

4 1/32 RACE CAR MECHANICS

Diverse cars like this Fly Panoz LMP Spyder roadster, Scalextric Cadillac Northstar LMS, Carrera BMW V12LMR, and Fly Viper can be made equal in performance so they can race in the same class.

Model car racing is supposed to be about how the car looks more than how it runs; even though these are, after all, racing cars and they are expected to race and–for some of us–to at least be capable of winning. You can certainly tune and adjust any model car chassis and, in truth, some maintenance is essential. If you are as much a builder as an admirer of model cars, you can build a model of just about any real car using existing chassis and clear plastic or cast-resin bodies.

1/32-Scale Race Car Chassis Design

Today, 1/32-scale ready-to-race cars are available in several chassis configurations. Often the location of the motor is governed by a need to have a full driver figure in the car. That means the model car's motor is in the same front or rear location as the engine in the real car. This adds an interesting touch of mechanical realism to the model. There is no such thing as a standard chassis design, even for a specific brand. There are three "standard" chassis designs: the motor running the length of the chassis and posi-

Even cars with chassis as diverse as the gearless sidewinder in this Carrera Viper and the inline front motor chassis beneath this Fly Viper can be adjusted so both cars offer equal performance.

tioned as close as possible to the rear of the car is called an "Inline Rear"; the motor positioned along the length of the chassis but mounted near the front of the car with a short "driveshaft" to the rear axle is an "Inline Front"; and the motor positioned across the chassis parallel to the rear axle is a "Sidewinder." The inline designs use a small pinion gear to drive a crown gear on the axle. Most of the sidewinder designs use a similar pinion gear, but drive a conventional gear on the rear axle. Some of the older Carrera cars designed before 1999 have a rubber wheel instead of a gear that touches the rear tire for a direct drive from motor to tire.

Each type of chassis has unique performance characteristics but none of them is really "better" than the other. If you are racing different types of chassis in the same racing class, however, you may want to allow some adjustments, such as more or less magnetic force, or additional weight at the front or rear

There are four types of 1/32-scale chassis design (left to right): Inline Rear (from Ninco's Ferrari Testa Rossa), Inline Front (from MRRC's Chaparral), Sidewinder (from Fly's Lola T70 MkIIIB), and Sidewinder direct-drive (from Carrera's Porsche GT1).

to equalize the performance of different chassis on different tracks.

Tune-Ups

In model car racing, as in real racing, the term "tune up" means to check every component on the car to

be certain it is working precisely as it should. Start with the wheels and tires and check to see that no lint or hair is wound around the axles to cause friction. Clean out any dirt or lint with a pipe cleaner. Apply a single drop of plastic-compatible oil to each bearing

The MRRC Formula One and the CART chassis for open-wheeled race cars has two small magnets beside the gear and Scalextric Formula, and both have a wide rectangular magnet in front of the gear.

and wipe any excess oil away with a clean pipe cleaner or a piece of facial tissue wrapped around a toothpick. Clean the excess grease from the gear teeth, apply new plastic-compatible grease, and wipe away any extra.

Adjust the pickup braids on either side of the guide shoe so they are bent into a gentle ess curve and spaced to touch the pickup strips on your particular brand of track. Be sure the wires are connected tightly to the holes beside the pickup shoes. With Scalextric and SCX cars, be sure the guide shoe is snapped completely into the hole so it touches the metal strips to complete the electrical circuit to the motor.

Spin the front wheels to make sure the tires and wheels are round, and if necessary, use your fingers to bend the wheels gently until they are running true. Place the car on the track and lift the rear so you can apply enough throttle to gently spin the rear wheels to check them. The rear tires can be sanded into an even, round shape by holding a piece of fine-grit sandpaper face up on the track while you gently lower a running car onto the sandpaper. Finally, check to be sure the body fits properly so that there's no chance it can be rubbed by any of the tires.

Troubleshooting

The quickest way to tell if you have a problem with the car is to try another car on that lane. If that car does not run either, the problem probably lies in the controller, the connections from the controller to the track, the connections for the power pack to the track or wall socket, or in the track itself. The most common problem with

1/32-scale race cars is the metal braid on each side of the pickup or guide shoe that contacts the metal strips on the track. If you accidentally pull the car backward, the braid can become bent and it will no longer touch the pickup strips on the track properly. It is also common, particularly with Scalextric cars, for the guide shoe to twist so far to the side that it partially drops from the chassis. The solution is to push the guide shoe back into its hole. It is also possible the wires that connect to the guide shoe have broken or been disconnected, but the body must be removed in order to check them. Try the bare chassis before you replace the body. If the car still does not run, check the wire connections to the motor to be sure they are still in place. Finally, try connecting a motor from another car to the pickup or guide shoe of the "problem" car to see if the fault lies in the motor.

1/32-Scale Performance Parity

An enjoyable aspect of this hobby is making the cars' performance realistic relative to one another. Select the cars you want to compete in a given class using some of the reference material from chapters 3 and 13. Once the cars have

MRRC offers steering in their CART and early Formula One cars, as does SCX, but it really doesn't help the handling—it just looks great.

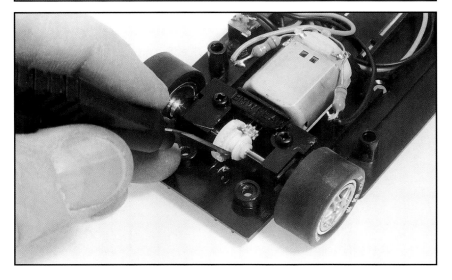

Top
Use a pipe cleaner to remove any dirt, lint, or excess grease or oil from the rear axle bearings.

Center
Remove any excess grease, hair, or lint from around the crown gear and pinion gear with a pipe cleaner.

Bottom
You many need to use a hobby knife to scrape away the excess lint or grease from the confined areas where the pinion and crown gears mesh.

been grouped, you'll soon discover that one will be considerably faster than the others. "Performance Parity" simply means that you are going to adjust the performance of the cars so all of them are as identical as you can get them, and that the races are won by either driver skill or luck, and not by "performance secrets."

The Fly and MRRC ready-to-run cars usually have the strongest magnets and the most powerful motors. The SCX cars have strong magnets, but the motors are not as strong as those in the Fly or MRRC cars. Replacement magnets are available for just about any car, and accessory magnets are available from Slot–It, Pro-Slot, Ninco, Carrera, and Fly. In this example you have the choice of either replacing the magnets in the Fly, MRRC, and SCX cars with weaker magnets or adding stronger magnets to all the other cars. A third choice is to remove the magnets from all of your cars. There are many model car racers who do that so the drivers who win races are the ones who have the best driving skills.

Real Racing "Downforce"
The concept of using wind generated by the moving car to create a "downforce" has changed real racing in the past 30 years. Airplane designers knew that an airfoil would produce lift, but it took another 50 years before race car designers completely understood the effect could be inverted to produce downforce.

The downforce effect has made the Prototype Sports, GT, Formula One, IRL, CART cars, and production sedans run faster. In fact, the Ford, Chevrolet, Pontiac, and Dodge stock cars have been subtly reshaped and redesigned so they all have equal downforce.

Many of today's 1/32-scale cars have captured the effects of aerodynamic downforce using an entirely different physical principle: magnetism. Most of the 1/32-scale cars are now fitted with small magnets on the bottom of the car that grip the steel pickup strips on the track. Each brand of car has magnets of different strengths, and different magnets are fitted to different cars of the same brand. There is a vast span of magnetic force that ranges from the very subtle force on the Scalextric Formula One cars and most of the Carrera cars, to the extremely strong magnetic force of the Fly, SCX, and MRRC ready-to-run cars.

The good news is that magnetic force is adjustable. You can add or subtract magnetic force by adding or subtracting magnets. However, changing the magnets does more than just change the grip–it changes how the car feels. You can actually adjust the force so the car leaves the track tail first (oversteer) or nose first (understeer).

The gear-driven Carrera cars have magnets that can be adjusted

by moving them back and forth in a slot. A tilted steel plate holds the magnet in position with the forward end of the plate being higher than the rear. For maximum traction, push the magnet toward the center of the car; for less traction, push the magnet forward.

The real cars made before 1970 had very little in the way of aerodynamic downforce, so you may want to consider removing the magnets from any models of 1970 or earlier cars. However, the real race cars from the last 10 years have a considerable amount of aerodynamic downforce, so you might consider increasing the magnetic force in models of more modern cars.

Increasing "Downforce"

In most cases, changing magnets is a matter of experimenting with different brands of magnets in different locations. MRRC, for instance, places very strong magnets near the middle of the car while Fly places magnets near the rear of the car. You may need to try different magnets and locations until you find the best combination for that particular car. You can remove the magnets from any of the 1/32-scale model cars by simply prying them loose with a screwdriver. Sometimes the stronger magnet will fit in the same place. In some cases, you can simply stack a stronger magnet on top of the original magnet if you

Left
If the guide shoe is too deep, you can slice 1/32 inch from the bottom with a hobby knife.

Below
The pickup braids on either side of the guide shoe must be clean and bent slightly downward so they contact the pickup strips for their full length when the car is on the track. Be sure they are spread properly from side to side so they contact the pickup strips on the track.

want to increase the magnetic downforce of the car. You can also increase the magnetic downforce by fitting smaller diameter tires or sanding down the stock tires. Conversely, you can decrease the magnetic downforce by fitting larger tires.

If you are installing new magnets in a new location, you will want to get the magnets as close to the pickup strips as possible. You may also want to have the magnets spaced at least 1/16-inch farther apart than the pickup strips to minimize the grip of the magnets on the straights. You can cut holes in the chassis with a motor tool or drill bit to open each corner, and then connect the drilled holes with a hobby knife. The magnets can be held in place with epoxy.

Be careful with powerful magnets. Keep them away from anything that can be affected by strong magnetic force, including CDs, computers, watches, credit cards, and pacemaker heart-enhancing devices.

Changing the Weight Distribution

You may be able to achieve extra traction or balance from some of the cars by adding more weight to the chassis. If the car runs great almost everywhere but seems to have a tendency to pop out of the slot more than others (particularly coming down from a bridge), consider adding a half-ounce or a quarter

ounce of weight close to the front axle. Similarly, cars that seem a bit tail-heavy and slide out more than similar cars can be improved by adding a half-ounce or an ounce of weight somewhere near the rear axle. Stores that sell automobile tires have stick-on lead weights, usually in 1/4-ounce and larger sizes. Handle the lead carefully to avoid lead poisoning.

Balancing Motors, Magnets, and Controllers

The motor in the car may not be strong enough to propel a car with its increased magnetic force. Faster and more powerful motors are available for any ready-to-run model car. For example, Ninco offers the faster NC-2 motor as a replacement for the NC-1 that is fitted to some of their less-expensive cars. This is also a faster motor than the motor in the SCX cars. The SCX 50120 Pro Turbo motor or the Playfit Rabbit motor provides performance similar to the Ninco NC-2. Any of these motors should offer better performance from an SCX or Artin car. To match these motors, you might want to try Slot-It, Tweaker, Carrera's 85039, Ninco's 70179, Pro-Track's PH1344, or Fly's B-21 magnets to replace or supplement the stock magnets in Ninco,

The magnets in the friction-drive Carrera cars can be moved from front to back by simply loosening a pair of screws, moving the magnets, and retightening the screws. The magnet on the newer gear-drive Carrera cars can be slid back for more traction, or forward for less traction without having to undo any screws.

Scalextric, Carrera, or Artin cars. You can go at least two stages faster with motors like Playfit's Fox or Cheetah, but you will need a power pack with at least 1/2 amp per lane, and you may need a controller with 5, 10, or 20 ohms to be able to control the more powerful cars. These last two motors and the controllers are more typical of the kinds of cars you'd find in use on one of the huge eight-lane commercial tracks.

When the strength of the magnets is increased, the motor is forced to work harder to propel the car down the track. The car may feel sluggish and may only move by using the last fraction of the trigger or push button's movement. If you have this kind of problem with the controller, the controller will have to be matched to the car, and the magnets matched to the motor. The controllers are rated in ohms and are matched to the cars in the set. You may find that you have more control of cars with more powerful motors like the Fly cars if you use a controller with a lower-than-standard ohm rating of 30 or 45 ohms. Ninco's Vario and Carrera's Xtreme-Control are two controllers with adjustable ohm ratings so the

controller can be used for any brand of car. Scalextric and SCX offer a 45-ohm controller, and Parma and MRRC offer controllers with 45 ohms, 25 ohms, and even less. You may want to try a different controller because you like the feel better. There's more information on controllers in chapter 12.

The power pack must have enough amps to feed the faster motors. For instance, if you race Fly cars on an Artin track, you will probably have to replace the Artin power pack with one from Carrera or Radio Shack that has more amps available to each lane, as suggested in chapter 12.

Better Tires and Wheels

The tires on your car are probably as good as you'll get. However, some older tires may have become hard enough to offer less-than-optimum traction. You can usually buy replacement tires from the importer or manufacturer of your car. New Indy Grips or similar tires are molded from silicone rubber. These silicone tires offer perhaps the best performance, but they are not always an improvement over the stock tires. Possibly the greatest advantage in

trying silicone tires is that you'll know if you're getting the maximum performance from your stock tires. You will also know if you want to make silicone tires acceptable replacements for any races. The silicone tires are available to fit any stock wheel. The cars that are raced on the eight-lane commercial tracks are usually fitted with foam rubber tires. These tires can be used on a plastic track, but they really are not worth the bother and make the best models look like toys.

Silicone tires can be easily split when attempting to mount them on the wheels. To minimize the risk of splitting, lubricate the tire with water, then use light finger pressure to push the tire onto the wheel by prying it over the wheel's edge just 1/8-inch at a time.

If you are having trouble with non-round wheels and cannot bend them straight with hand pressure, you may want to consider using wheels from another brand. Scalextric, Ninco, Fly, MRRC, and Carrera offer complete replacement front or rear axles that include tires. EJ's, MRRC, Pattos, Slot–It, and others offer replacement aluminum wheels, axles, and gears. You may need to remove the wheels from your axles to utilize the bearings for a replacement axle. It's usually possible to pull the first wheel from the axle by hand, but you'll need to grip the axle with pliers to remove the second wheel. Just be sure the pliers are holding a part of the axle that will not be inside the bearing when the assembly is installed in the car. Ninco's 70201 Gear Puller is designed to remove and replace wheels and gears on both the motor and axle. You can use a vise to reassemble the wheels, but you'll need a 2-inch piece of 1/8-inch inside diameter tubing to use a spacer to get a replacement gear into place. The Ninco Gear Puller can be used for this same task.

Racing Secrets

It is certainly possible to build a better 1/32-scale car than the out-of-the-box models, but this hobby

Indy Grips and others make replacement silicone tires for virtually any 1/32-scale wheel including (left to right) Scalextric Formula One cars, MRRC (ex-Airfix) 1960s-era Formula One cars, MRRC's Clubman chassis, and the Monogram/Revell/Cox-style aluminum wheels available from EJ's Hobbies.

is about realistic racing, not performance. In fact, I strongly recommend you do everything possible to be sure the performance of all the cars is equal within each racing class. There are, however, a few performance areas you will want to check every time you race:

- Be sure the tires are all round and touching the track.
- Be sure the pickup guide is free to pivot without binding.
- Adjust the guide shoe so it does not stick to either side when the car comes out of the slot.
- Be sure the pickup braid is touching the pickup strips on the track.
- Be sure that there's no more than a paper-thickness of sideways movement of either the front or rear axles and that they cannot touch the body.
- Oil the bearings, grease the gears, and wipe away any excess oil or grease.

A vise can also be used to press new wheels onto axles.

The Ninco 70201 Gear Puller can be used to remove wheels and crown gears from axles and pinion gears from motors. It can also be used as a press to install wheels, crown gears, and pinion gears.

5

BUILD YOUR OWN RACE CARS

I wasn't as pleased as I'd hoped with the wire wheel-conversion I'd made on the Lotus 7 so I went for the Minilites. Scalextric only offers the Caterham with Minilites but the wheels and axles are available so I fitted them to the Lotus 7.

The ready-to-run electric race car models are nearly exact replicas of real cars that ran in a specific race, right down to the sponsor decals, and the proper car color and number. There's usually not much you can do to increase the realism of these cars other than paint the driver's helmet to match the actual driver (and that's often already done for you). You can, however, change the numbers and decals to match another car, or repaint the car and apply decals to match a car that competed in another race. You can even build your own car from a kit or from component parts like cast-resin or clear plastic bodies and chassis from existing racers or all-metal chassis.

New Paint and Numbers

It is sometimes possible to remove the factory numbers with an alcohol-soaked cotton swab. If that doesn't work, try lacquer thinner and rub gently enough to remove the numbers but not the paint. Do not expect success unless you are very lucky. You will likely need to repaint and decal the complete car, but it's worth a try. Be sure to work outdoors or in a well-ventilated area when using alcohol, thinners, lacquers, or any other flammable materials.

Scalextric's LeMans Cadillac Northstar LMS, Fly's Panoz Spyder roadster, and Carrera's 1999 LeMans-winning BMW V12 LMR are state-of-the-art cars. All have full interior detailing with a complete driver figure and near-perfect detail and markings.

It is possible to repaint a model with spray cans or a brush, but I do not recommend it. If you want a finish that is at least as good as the factory cars from Fly, Ninco, Scalextric, Carrera, and MRRC, an airbrush is about the only way to achieve it. The airbrush also allows you to use genuine factory-matched lacquer paints from Model Car World (MCW) so you can have the correct car colors. Any enamel or model paint can be used, but the MCW lacquer covers well with a thin coat. Apply a coat of primer first to seal the body and provide a base for the final color coat.

How to Apply Decals

Decals are available from Pattos, MRE, MRRC, EJ's, Pro-Slot, Slixx, and others to match specific real race cars. MRE, for example, offers the square-style numbers favored by Ferrari in the 1960s. To apply decals, first dip the decal in water for about 10 seconds and set the decal on a piece of facial tissue to allow the water to soak through the paper to the decal's glue. When you can move the decal on the paper, position both the decal and paper where you want it on the model and gently slide the paper from beneath the decal with tweezers. Apply Microscale Micro-Sol or Testors Model Masters Decal Solvent on the decal so it can conform to the surface. Apply the fluid while the decal is still wet and let it dry overnight. When the decal work is finished, gently clean away any solvent or cement with a damp tissue and let the model dry. Finally, spray the model with Testors Model Master Gloss Finish. Other clear paints might work as well, but they tend to be too thick for 1/32-scale models.

Do-It-Yourself Detail

The original Scalextric cars of the 1950s and 1960s were mostly 1/29 scale, as were the out-of-production Strombecker D-Type Jaguar and Testa Rossa Ferrari models. The Ninco XK120 Jaguar, a current example, is 1/32 scale but it is approximately a scale foot (about 3/8-inch) wider than it would be if it were an exact scale model. The extra width makes the car more competitive as a model race car than if it were the exact-scale width. Personally, I intend to take the Ninco chrome parts, chassis, wheels, and interior and graft them onto an old Revell "Highway Pioneers" (now made by Dapol) exact-1/32-scale Jaguar XK120 display-model body.

Since many of these cars are sold to children, they do not usually have the tobacco or alcohol-related sponsor decals. However, you can buy replacement decals for Marlboro from Pro-Slot, and West decals for F1 McLarens from Pattos.

The 1/32-scale cars can be customized to create cars you wanted to buy but couldn't afford in real life. The red Lotus 7 has the stock Scalextric replicas of some type of stamped-steel disc wheels that were apparently fitted to some Lotus 7s. I wanted a Lotus 7 with wire wheels so I adapted a set of Ninco's to this model.

This Scalextric Aston Martin was first released in the 1960s, then re-released in the 1990s. It has the typical molded-color plastic "toy" look of many early slot cars.

The stock wire wheels of the Scalextric Aston Martin were replaced with Ninco wire wheels, tires, axles, and gears. The wheels fit fine, but they lowered the car so much that the guide shoe had to be replaced with Ninco's guide shoe.

Similarly, the body on the Ninco Ferrari Testa Rossa is about a scale 6 inches too thick. I removed the body, filed off 1/8 inch from the joining seams and interior, pushed the sides in for more roll-under, painted the chassis black to disguise its width, and repainted the model to match Phil Hill's 1958 Targa Florio car. Does it matter? No, but I want my models to be in the proper proportion to one another. If I discover that an exact-scale car cannot compete with a larger model car, I'll simply build another replica of a similar small car to compete with the exact-scale car.

You can improve the realism of many model cars by accenting the panel lines that indicate the edges of the hood, doors, and trunk. Gently slice along the molded-in lines with a hobby knife. Then use a No. 00-size brush to flow a thin bead of waterproof black ink into the sliced lines. Use a damp cloth to wipe off the ink before it dries. The result is a hairline black line comparable to the Carrera Maserati A6GCS and the modified Ninco Ferrari Testa Rossa.

Models from Toys

If you are willing to do some actual modeling, you can upgrade many of the toy cars of today and apply the same technique to upgrade some of the older toy cars. I discovered that the Scalextric Aston Martin, which has been reproduced several times, was very close to being precisely 1/32 scale. It just looked like a toy because that's the kind of car Scalextric was producing in the 1970s and 1980s. I wanted a scale model, so I disassembled the car and fitted Ninco wire wheels for appearance and to lower the car. I then used the lower-profile Ninco guide shoe, which meant I also needed to cut a large crescent-shaped swatch of plastic from the chassis to clear the Ninco guide. There was little plastic left to support the guide pivot post, so I reinforced it with metal-filled epoxy. Finally, the car was

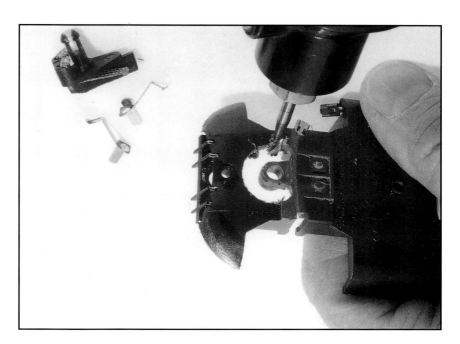

Use a milling bit in a motor tool to cut the crescent-shaped clearance slot so the Ninco guide shoe can be used in the modified Scalextric Aston Martin.

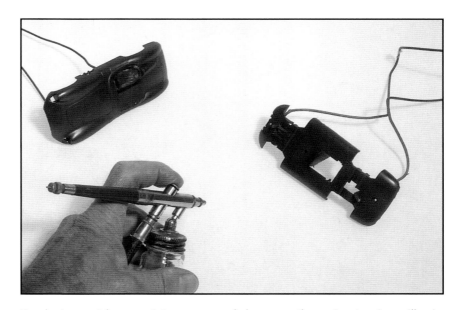

Bend wire coat hangers into ampersand shapes so the spring tension will grip inside the body, and then spray paint the body with an airbrush.

painted with an exact match for one of the Aston Martin greens from MCW (*Model Car World*). It is numbered to match the car Stirling Moss drove in the 1958 Targa Florio, one of the few times he competed directly with Phil Hill.

Assembling and Painting Cast-Resin Kits

Top-Slot, Slot Classic, Any Slot, Speed Cast, and Etzel are firms that offer cast-resin body kits designed to screw onto the existing plastic chassis. You may find other

The Scalextric Aston Martin has been lowered and rebuilt with Ninco wire wheels, tires, gears, and guide shoe. The Testa Rossa Ferrari is a Ninco model repainted and decaled. The models are re-creations of cars that raced in the 1958 Targa Florio road race. The Aston Martin is a replica of the car driven by Stirling Moss, and the Ferrari is a replica of the car driven by Phil Hill.

The rebuilt Scalextric Aston Martin and Ninco Testa Rossa Ferrari with other out-of-the-box vintage racers are shown. Also included is Carrera's replica of the 1955 Mille Miglia-winning Mercedes 300SLR, which was also driven by Moss. Carrera's Maserati A6GCS from the 1953 Mille Miglia (an A6GCS No. 621 won its class in the 1955 Mlle Miglia, but Carrera has not offered that paint scheme), Scalextric's Lotus 7 (with Minilite wheels from a Caterham), and Ninco's XK120 Jaguar are also shown.

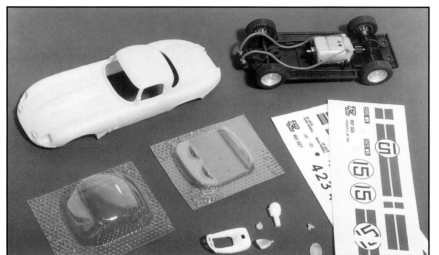

Top

The Ninco Ferrari Testa Rossa out-of-the-box (21) compared to a modified version with linked-in panel lines (98). The Carrera A6GCS has been modified by lowering the body 1/16 inches and using paint to fill in spaces in the grill and exhaust pipes, and create panel lines.

Center

The Top Slot kits include a cast-resin body, vacuum-formed clear plastic window, and interior driver figure and decals to match the specific prototype car. This Top Slot replica of the Lightweight Jaguar E-Type has the precise details found on the Cunningham and Qvale cars and both sets of decals are included in the kit. An MRRC Chaparral chassis, motor, and guide shoe, and Ninco Porsche front and rear axles and wheels will also need to be purchased.

Bottom

The Top Slot replica of the Cobra Daytona Couple includes decals for a half-dozen cars. To assemble the model, remove any rough flash for the edges of the windows and wheel openings with a jeweler's file, paint the model with an airbrush, and apply decals.

firms if you search. The cast-resin is nowhere near as strong as injection-molded plastic, but you can reinforce it with epoxy. The sole advantage of cast-resin bodies is that they allow you to build cars you cannot buy as ready-builts. The cast-resin body kits are usually better-detailed than the clear plastic bodies.

To assemble the kits, clean away any mold flash from around the windows, wheel arches, and other openings with a jeweler's file. I recommend that you fill in the area around the body mounting posts with a thick fillet of epoxy putty. Test-fit the body on the chassis to be sure the putty does not interfere with the motor, axles, or other parts of the chassis. Fit the windows and interior but do not install them until after the body is painted.

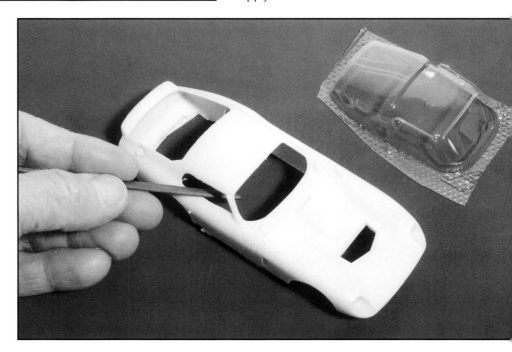

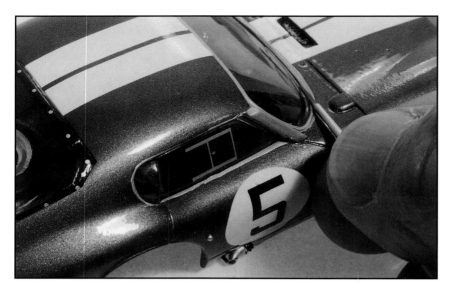

Wash the body thoroughly in detergent, rinse, and let it air dry. I recommend an airbrush for painting cast-resin bodies because you can obtain a smoother and more even finish with less paint, and you have the opportunity to select actual race car colors in lacquer rather than enamel. Paint the body, apply decals, and use a No. 00 brush to add the final details such as window frames and door handles. Spray the model with Testors Model Master Clear Gloss, and install the windows, interior, and any clear parts, including headlight lenses or taillights. The last step is to mount the body on the chassis that is suggested by the body maker.

Use the side of a No. 00 paintbrush to paint the windows. It's best to paint the frames before you install the clear plastic windows.

Use five-minute epoxy to install the windows and clear headlight lenses on the Top Slot body.

The Top Slot body includes mounting posts to fit the MRRC Chaparral chassis. I would strongly recommend you reinforce the Top Slot body-mounting posts with epoxy putty.

Some of the 1/32-scale chassis currently available include (left to right): EJ's No. 2GC (with Fox motor and EJ's aluminum wheels, matching tires, axles, and gears and guide shoe); MRRC's No. 9980 Clubman (with their 9981 Handling Set, 9982 Screws Set, 9984 Braid Set, 9985 Gear, 9986 Magnets, 9987 Clubman Motor, 9988 axles and bearings, 9989 aluminum front wheels and tires, and 9990 aluminum rear wheels and tires); Playfit 94801 Chassis (complete, less motor, the motor is a Fox with Playfit crown gear and pinion); and a Pro-Track No. 340 Spyder chassis (complete, less motor, the motor is a Playfit Rabbit).

The Parma No. 574 Excalibur chassis (left) can be adapted to a number of different motors including Ninco's NC-2 using the Ninco 70127 Ninco motor-mounting bracket. It also fits Ninco wheels such as these from the Cobra. The body-mounting posts are designed so the motor can be used beneath most Ninco bodies, but it can be adapted to other brands as well. The EJ's No. 2GC (with a Fox motor and EJ's aluminum wheels, matching tires, axles and gears, and pickup guide) includes body-mounting bracket and locations to allow it to be used under Ninco and other plastic bodies as well as clear plastic bodies. The brackets are EJ's to adapt this chassis to just about any motor.

The Top Slot Lightweight E-Type and Daytona Cobra Coupe with a Revell (a near-identical model is available for Pink-Kar) Ferrari GTO and MRRC's Cobra.

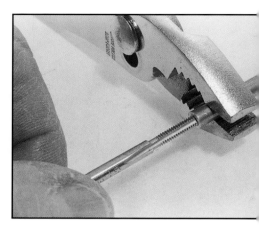

You can make your own mounting brackets for injection-molded plastic, cast-resin, or clear plastic bodies from K & S No. 3060 aluminum tubing. Use a 4-40 tap held in a pin vise to thread the tube, then use 4-40 screws to mount the post to the chassis, and epoxy the post to the body.

Build Your Own Race Car

You can assemble your own 1/32-scale models using either a plastic chassis from MRRC, Ninco, Carrera, or Fly, or by using one of the metal aftermarket chassis from Pro-Track, MRRC, EJ's, Playfit, or Parma. All of these chassis have some provision to adapt body-mounting, but you usually have to provide the body-mounting posts or plates. The metal chassis are another of those "love it or hate it" items; some racers adapt their favorite metal chassis to Fly, Ninco, or Scalextric bodies and scrap the chassis just to get the body. Other racers prefer to adapt Ninco, Fly, or MRRC chassis to clear plastic or cast-resin bodies so the custom-built cars perform like the factory-built models.

Cast-resin bodies are also available from Classic and Nostalgia. These two firms offer a vast range of bodies, mostly from the 1950s to 1970s. These bodies must be trimmed along the lower edges and the windows removed. EJ's, Betta, and Pattos offer wide ranges of clear plastic bodies. Be prepared to be either thrilled or disappointed with the clear plastic body. Some are almost as good as cast-resin bodies (many appear to be made from the same cast-resin body molds), but some are just "blobs" and many are too wide or large to be scale models. The quality does not vary much between identical models of the same car from the same company, so the problem is not quality control but just poorly made original molds. Before you spend lots of time building the model, do some research to determine the exact dimensions of the real car you want to model, and research two or three other cars so you have some alternatives. None of the bodies are guaranteed to be a precise scale and they are not returnable, so you take a chance. The good news is that

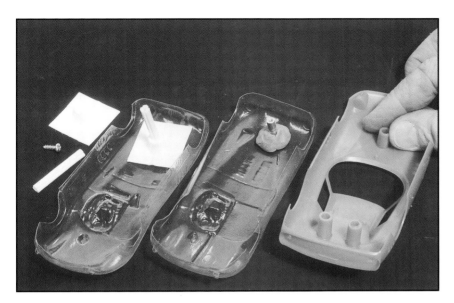

Pattos offers a vacuum-formed post and pad (right) that makes it easy to mount clear plastic (shown) or cast-resin bodies to either metal or plastic chassis. If you make your own posts from K & S aluminum tube and 4-40 screws, you can mount the post to the body with epoxy putty (center). The factory-produced injection-molded bodies include mounting posts such as those inside this MRRC Ferrari GTO/LM (right).

Three alternate methods of mounting clear plastic or cast-resin bodies to metal chassis. Rocky Russo uses 3/8-inch square strips of bass wood and solders brass brackets to the sides of the chassis like this out-of-production Pittman motor and Atlas chassis. EJ's No. 2A inline chassis is similar. The Playfit 9801 chassis (center) has aluminum plates designed to be epoxied inside the body and attached (and removed) to the chassis with small screws. The Pro-Track chassis (left) has unique 1/4-inch aluminum tacks that are to be epoxied inside the body. The body can be removed by spreading it slightly so the tacks pop out of the plastic tubes extending from the sides of the Pro-Track chassis.

they are very inexpensive so you can justify buying four or five bodies to find the one that is the right size for 1/32 scale and that has acceptable detail.

You can "sample" this segment of the hobby by buying one of the complete car kits with an injection-molded plastic body and metal chassis from MRRC or EJ's. Currently, MRRC offers a series of 1964 Ferrari 250 GTO/LM bodies from the 1970s-era Monogram molds on their own Clubman chassis, and EJ's has the original Volkswagen Beetle on their 2GC-series chassis.

Painting Clear Plastic Bodies

Clear plastic bodies are used almost exclusively on the cars that are raced on the huge eight-lane commercial tracks. These bodies are painted on the inside so the clear plastic protects the paint. However, the thick layer of plastic makes the model look toylike. The clear plastic stands up to the high-speed crashes better than any other plastic or cast-resin, but it doesn't have as much detail as injection-molded plastic or cast-resin. You can build a realistic car using a clear plastic body, but you must paint the body on the outside to match the realism of the Fly, Ninco, Carrera, and Scalextric cars. You must also be willing to use separate detail parts from the ready-built cars. The clear plastic bodies must be trimmed by the modeler to open up the wheel arches and cockpits. I use a Dremel motor tool with a No. 194 milling bit. The motor tool and bit allow me to have very precise control over how much material I remove. I've tried knives, files, and scissors to trim clear plastic bodies, but none work as well for me as the motor tool and milling bit.

Car Wash and Polish

The finish on most of the ready-to-run model cars is already protected with a coat of clear paint. The clear paint is just paint and it will become scratched as the car slides across the track on its roof because you didn't brake soon

This Betta clear plastic body has been painted and decaled on the outside to match the quality of today's out-of-the box racers.

To paint clear plastic bodies on the outside, use a liquid masking fluid like Microscate's Micro-Mask to protect the windows. Spray the body with primer, followed by the proper color coats.

enough. Protect the car's finish with a thick coat of Future-brand clear acrylic floor protection, paste floor wax like Simonize or use real automobile wax such as Turtle Wax.

Never use a solvent of any kind to clean a car and be wary of heavy-duty cleaners. Plain soap and water will usually remove the scuffs and smears. For the worst scratches, spray a little WD-40 on a clean, soft rag and polish the area, wash it with soap and water, rinse, dry, and apply the protective wax.

Any of these 1/32-scale cars can be raced on any of the 1/32-scale tracks that are shown in this book. The cars are just a part of the hobby. The real fun begins when you see these realistic race car models in motion.

6

1/32-SCALE TRACK

Steve Burkey assembled some of the MRRC (ex-Airfix) 5064 Racing Pits and 5063 Press Box kits for this scene. The 1964 250GTO Ferrari is also an MRRC model assembled from their kit.

The cars are the main attraction to the hobby. The fact that they can actually be raced is a bonus beyond belief. You will discover that designing, building, and driving on 1/32-scale race tracks is the best possible way to enjoy the cars. The manufacturers have made it easy by designing sectional plastic tracks that are easily assembled and disassembled. The track designs are each based on a workable and changeable geometry so you can create a complex track and still have every joint fit securely.

Most of us get into this model car racing hobby by buying a figure-8 set with two cars. There's no

better way to start because the combination of track, cars, controllers, and power supply is usually about half the cost of buying these components separately. The power supply is at least adequate for the cars, and the controllers are matched to the power needs of the motors and magnets in the cars.

How Much Does It Cost?

I'm not going to focus much on price because it can vary considerably depending on whether you buy the track as part of a set, if it's available in bulk, and how much is needed. Generally, Ninco and SCX are the most expensive, followed by

A Pro-Slot 1999 Ferrari F1 and a Ninco Stewart snake through the ess bends on the Scalextric 5 x 9 "Ascari" track. The red and white triangles are the Scalextric borders for their outer curve tracks.

Scalextric and Carrera. Artin is about half the price, but you need to buy an entire set to get the lowest price.

Track to Last a Lifetime

All of the 1/32-scale sectional plastic tracks are designed to accept any 1/32-scale race car. Some of the cars have deeper guide shoes than others and may need to be trimmed for some tracks. However, be sure you have the brand of track you intend to keep before you trim the guide shoe because it may not be necessary if you change brands.

There is little interchangeability between brands of tracks, but there are a few exceptions to the rule. Scalextric and SCX are virtually interchangeable. Ninco offers an adapter track to fit their track to Scalextric and SCX, but it won't work with a four-lane track or straight borders, and it can make it very difficult to arrange a track with both brands. The SCX and Scalextric controllers will plug into each other's connector track, but Ninco, Carrera, and Artin all have plugs that differ from any other brand except their own.

When looking for a brand of track, do not assume you have bought the "best" track until you have a chance to read everything in this book and can at least see a sample of the alternate brands. Far too many hobbyists have bought more and more track to match the track in the set only to discover that there is a better track out there. Consider the track, controllers, and power pack included in the first set to be part of the cost of learning about the hobby. Yes, you may keep the track and the controllers and the power supply forever because they work for you, but it's false economy to keep buying more of something that really doesn't satisfy you if you know there's something better. All of the 1/32-scale tracks, controllers, and power supplies are rugged enough to last a lifetime, so don't expect to wait until they are worn out to buy something better.

Scalextric Track

Scalextric is the best-known brand of model car racing track and the oldest that is still in production. In many parts of the world, the very word "Scalextric" has come to mean model car racing. No other firm offers the variety of track sections that Scalextric offers, although some track sections, such as banked turns, are available in very limited sizes only. Scalextric is the smallest track and most flexible, so it is well-suited for children in the 8- to 12-year-old range. Since the track is so easily disassembled, it is a good choice for those who like to build new tracks or who must take-up the track from the floor or ping-pong table when it is not in use. Scalextric, SCX, and Ninco use a "30-degree" geometry for the curves, and 12 sections are needed to complete a circle.

The track's flexibility and the large number of track sections required can make it seem rather "lumpy" to a serious racer, but real-world tracks from the 1950s and 1960s were even lumpier. The lanes are spaced somewhat closer together than with a Ninco or Carrera track, but that is only a problem if you are running some of the cars with a wider-than-accurate scale such as SCX's and Ninco's Grand Prix cars, where the wheels can tangle if the cars are wiggling too much down the straightaways. The only short-comings that are significant with Scalextric are that they do not offer an outer-outer curve, and the borders do not grip tight enough to be used effectively on overpass bridges or on carpet. The track does not fit together very tightly side-to-side when a four- or six-lane track is assembled, and it can only be held together with separate clips from Ninco. That's partially a result of the very flexibility that is one of the track's advantages. Because of that flexibility, you can often insert one of the shortest Scalextric No. C157 straight track sections to expand the inner two-lane sections so they are forced closer to the outer two-lane sections. The lanes are spaced 3 inches apart.

The borders Scalextric offers for their standard curve tracks are the most realistic you can buy, with a red and white "rumble" strip, a beige color to look like sand, and steel-colored guardrails that look like the Armco rails on real tracks. Scalextric also offers a "transition" straight that will direct any fishtailing cars straight by forcing them to bang against the guardrails if they are moving too far out. The bad news is that Scalextric does not offer this border for their outer curves. The borders for the outer curves are wide enough, but are a garish white with red triangles. They are too flexible to hold the paint that is applied and are difficult to repaint. I suggest painting them anyway using the techniques described later in this chapter. Also, they only accept the older-style single-rail guardrails.

Scalextric's greatest virtues, in my opinion, are the well thought out C8066 Power Plus connector track with built-in reversing switches and brake control, the C8045 Electronic Lap Counter and Timer, and the C8003 Pacer System to allow you to race against yourself. All three items are described in chapters 12 and 13. The reversing switch allows you to race cars in either direction without the need to remove the connector track and turn it around. Ninco's terminal track also has reversing switches and Carrera has reversing switches on the bottom of each of their cars.

SCX Track

The SCX track is completely interchangeable with Scalextric. The loops that connect the track sections have a slightly different shape, but they work on essentially the same principle and all of the track sizes are the same. SCX track has a considerably rougher texture that is very much like Ninco's. This is something you eiths roll rather than slide around the curves. SCX does not offer the range of accessory tracks of Scalextric, but they do have some unusual options like a chicane track

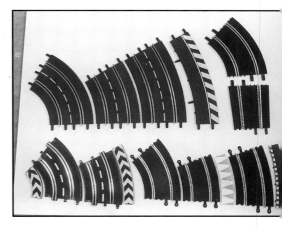

Examples of the five most popular brands of 1/32-scale track include (clockwise from upper left): Carrera standard, outer, and outer-outer curves, and outer-outer borders; Ninco standard curve with Ninco-to-Scalextric or SCX adapter; SCX outer-outer curve with border, Scalextric outer border, outer and standard curve; and Artin outer border, outer curve, standard curve, and inner curve border.

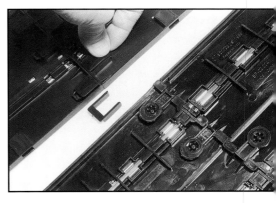

Scalextric (right) uses a system of tabs with built-in loops that lock over round pegs to hold their track sections together. Carrera (left) has a tab-and-slot assembly system with these U-shaped clips to lock the track securely together.

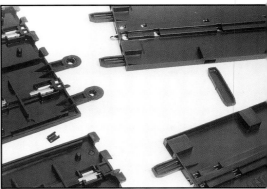

Use the Ninco 10213 metal clips to hold SCX track and the similar Scalextric (left) track sections together side-by-side to assemble four-lane tracks. Carrera (right) uses a plastic tab similar to their track joint tab to hold the four-lane tracks in side-by-side alignment so the Carrera 85010 metal clips are seldom needed.

The Riggen (left) and Strombecker/Bachmann standard curves.

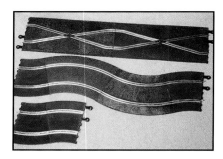

Two crossing sections joined end-to-end produce an interesting ess bend that makes it look like one of the two cars is attempting to stop the other from passing. Gentle ess bends made from two sections of Scalextric standard curves and two half-standard curves can be used to replace two straight track sections on any Scalextric or SCX track. Two half-standard curves (bottom) can sometimes be used to help join self-designed tracks not quite in alignment.

(with a chicane curve) with non-magnetic rails to provide a "slick" simulation of a rain-soaked corner.

The pros and cons for the Scalextric track are virtually the same for the SCX track in part because the tracks are nearly identical. The major disadvantage to SCX is that their borders are too narrow to be of much use. The most important advantage of SCX is that they offer the outer-outer curve that is so badly needed in the Scalextric system. Unfortunately, the SCX borders for their own outer-outer curve are too narrow.

The SCX borders are green with white and red "rumble" strips, and are packed in sets of six inner and outer strips for all the SCX and Scalextric curves. The borders look great and were, in part, the inspiration for the custom-painted Carrera borders.

Ninco Track

Ninco's track is a development of the Scalextric line to better suit serious racers. The lanes are spaced about a half-inch farther apart so the modern cars don't have a chance to nerf one another on the straights or curves. Ninco offers a full range of inner, standard, outer, and outer-outer curves, each with optional inside and outside borders. You can essentially build any track designed for Scalextric or SCX with Ninco. The broader 3-1/2-inch lane spacing simply means that the Ninco track requires more space. Ninco has a connection system very similar to the Scalextric and SCX system, but the loops require more pressure to engage, which makes it less likely they will accidentally disengage if the track is moved. Ninco does offer an adapter track to mate it to Scalextric or SCX, but the track is only useful for two-lanes and it can be difficult to fit some of the more complex tracks. My advice would be to pick one brand and sell or swap the mismatched track.

The primary disadvantage of Ninco's track is the rough surface. As with SCX, which has a similarly rough texture, you either love it or hate it. The Ninco borders are similar to the older Scalextric with garish white and red rectangles. Ninco offers electronic lap counters that can be used with their track as well as any other. One very nice feature about Ninco is that their controllers all have built-in brakes and the connector or terminal track has reversing switches as a standard fitting.

Carrera Track

The Carrera track has been available for about 15 years, but the price has recently been reduced to be equal or below that of the other brands. Carrera's track has a unique tab-and-slot assembly system with separate U-shaped locks that hold the track securely. The Carrera track is made of conventional hard plastic much like the original Revell, Monogram, and Strombecker tracks, but it is easier to assemble. The locking clips allow you to assemble the track into modules of 180-degree curves to make it easier to store the track without completely disassembling it. Carrera uses the same tab-and-slot system to attach the borders so they become an integral part of the track. Carrera also provides a double-ended tab and a metal clip to lock four or six lanes of track together side-by-side. The tabs are also used to attach the borders.

The 4-inch lane spacing on the Carrera track is wide enough for the models of the newest Formula One, Sports, and GT cars, and the borders are wide enough to leave room for the cars to slide out and park themselves out of the way of oncoming cars. Carrera offers standard, outer, and outer-outer curves and a series of banked curves in standard, outer, and outer-outer sizes. Each style has its own fitted border as an option. The banked turns allow you to construct "three-dimensional" tracks with two-, four-, or six-lane 180-degree super speedway-style banked turns, as well as 90-degree banked turns like those on the Indianapolis 500 track. Corkscrew-style downhill turns like the one on the Laguna Seca Raceway can also be re-created. There are examples of all three of these options in chapters 7 and 8.

Artin Track

Artin is designed for the toy rather than the hobby market. The 1/32-scale Artin track and cars are included in this book because the track is quite sturdy, it interlocks reliably, and the cars are reasonable replicas that perform well enough, especially at their low price. However, the HO Artin track and cars are too toylike to compare to the other brands of HO-scale racers in this book. Artin also includes inner and outer borders or skid aprons, and most sets and borders lock firmly

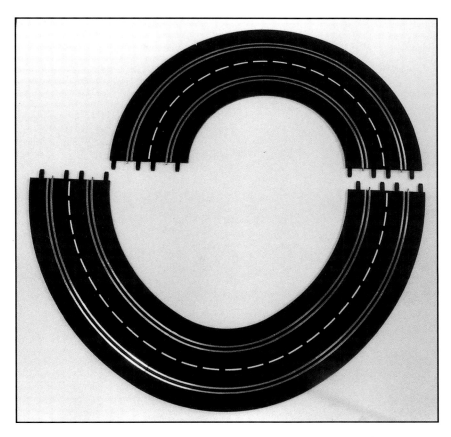

The top curve is assembled from three standard Carrera curves and the bottom curve is an increasing/decreasing radii turn made from two Carrera outer curves, a single standard curve, and two more outer curves.

you saw off the three 1/2-inch tabs from one end of the 60-degree section and cover the rails with the 1/4-inch pieces of metal rail that were cut. Cement the "new" half section to the end of the full-length section you just cut with metal-filled epoxy, then solder the pickup rail joints between the two pieces. Most track plans that require half curves usually link them to a full curve, so this custom-made 90-degree curve will be useful. Similarly, one or two 1/2-length straights can be cut and each can be added to another full-straight. When you assemble the extra-long straight in the track plan, you will need to add one full-length straight on the opposite side of the track to make up for the one-plus-1/4 (or 1/3 or 1/2) customized straight track. It's not easy, but the track is inexpensive.

Artin does offer the following replacement track sections:

- 5711 Straight Track
- 5712 60-Degree Inner Curve Track
- 5713 Crossover Track
- 5714 Banked Inner Curve Track
- 5717 Squeeze (chicane) Track
- 5716 15-Degree Outer Curve Track
- 57178 30-Degree Outer Curve Track

Artin does not offer any borders or skid aprons (that it calls "side curves") for the outside of the inner curves as accessory items. Borders for the inner curves can be obtained only by buying a two-lane set, and borders for the outer curves are only available by buying a four-lane set. There are no borders for the straight track sections, although short straight borders are included to transition from curve to straight. The easiest way to get straight borders would be to simply cut a piece of straight track in half and paint the two halves and curved borders as described for Carrera borders in this chapter.

Riggen, Bachmann, and Strombecker Track

Riggen is still producing brand-new sections of the Revell track from the 1970s. However, the

onto the track, which is unusual for a toy track, and it makes the Artin track far more fun to race on.

Artin offers by far the least-expensive sets, which means you can buy a four-lane set complete with cars for around $100 (as of 2001). The 1/32-scale Artin four-lane sets have been sold by J. C. Penney and some of the larger department stores in the East. However, none of these outlets carry extra track, cars, or parts. It can be difficult to obtain extra pieces of Artin track because few dealers carry it at the present time. Most Artin fans simply buy a "spare" four-lane set to obtain all of the track and replacement parts for the cars that they will ever need. You should be able to find a toll-free number for Artin in your set. If not, you may be able to locate a toll-free number by calling the Toy

Manufacturers of America office at (212) 675-1141.

Artin only offers 60-degree "Standard" curve track sections turns. They do not offer the 30-degree, 1/2-inner curve sections needed to make a 90-degree turn. An alternative would be to use all Artin "outer" curves from the four-lane set because those curves are 30 degrees. In fact, Artin has a 15-degree version of their outer curve. There are no borders for these half- and quarter-length outside curves, but it's easy enough to saw one of the outer borders to fit because the borders lock securely to the edge of the track regardless of their length.

Artin does not offer any 1-2-, 1/3-, or 1/4-length straight track sections, so you may be forced to cut those sections to fit a complete Artin layout. If you decide to cut Artin curve track sections, I suggest

The Pros and Cons of Picking the Best Track

Scalextric Track

Pros
- Easiest track to assemble and disassemble
- Because of the above, it is the best track for children
- Locks together well on a solid floor or tabletop
- Good compromise between too little and too much traction
- Best variety of track sections
- Cars are less noisy on this relatively soft track
- Flexible enough to allow some misalignment
- Flexible enough to allow slight banking in turns
- Great-looking borders for standard curves
- Borders for outer curves are wide enough
- Great-looking guardrails for standard curves
- Excellent low-cost lap counter/timers
- Plug-in option for reversing direction
- Highly recommended "Pacer" option to race against yourself
- Interchanges with SCX and can be adapted to Ninco

Cons
- Track comes apart too easily to be moved without complete disassembly
- Borders do not attach firmly enough for use on crossing bridges
- Must buy second transformer and connector track for individual power supply to each lane
- Slot too shallow for other brands of cars
- No outer-outer curves available
- Close lane spacing for modern Formula One and sports/GT cars
- No banked curves available
- Color of outer curve and straight borders not realistic

Ninco Track

Pros
- Track assembles easily and holds together well
- Offers outer-outer curves
- Slot deep enough to allow any brand of car to operate
- Cars are less noisy on this relatively soft track
- Flexible enough to allow some misalignment
- Flexible enough to allow some banking in turns
- Borders available for inside and outside of all curves
- Wide borders for outer curves
- Individual lane power standard
- Reversing standard
- Brake feature standard

Cons
- Rough track surface
- Can be difficult to find
- Can be expensive
- No banked track
- Color of borders not realistic
- No self-racing program track

Carrera Track

Pros
- Track holds together tightly enough to operate on carpet and to move easily
- Offers outer-outer curves
- Offers borders for all curves
- Borders are wide enough for any 1/32-scale car
- Offers banked turns
- Connector track has built-in brake feature
- Slot is deep enough for any brand of car
- Individual lane power standard
- Brakes standard

Cons
- Can be difficult for children under 12 to disassemble
- Plastic tabs can break off if track is carelessly disassembled
- Track can break if stepped on
- No reversing available
- Borders are black with "Construction Zone" yellow chevrons
- No self-racing program track

Artin Track

Pros
- Lowest cost
- Track locks together easily and firmly
- Borders attach easily and firmly

Cons
- Can be difficult for children under 12 to disassemble
- Plastic tabs can break off if track is carelessly disassembled
- Track can break if stepped on
- No reversing available
- Borders are black with "Construction Zone" yellow chevrons
- No self-racing program track

SCX Track

Pros
- Same as Scalextric
- Outer-outer lanes available
- Best-looking borders of all the tracks

Cons
- Same as Scalextric
- Rough track surface
- Borders are too narrow to be really useful
- Can be difficult to find
- Can be expensive
- Must use Scalextric track section for individual lane power supply
- No reversing available
- No self-racing program track

Riggen or Strombecker/Bachmann Track

Pros
- Locks together tightly
- Wide lane spacing

Cons
- Can be difficult for children under 12 to disassemble
- No half-inner curves available
- No half straights available
- No borders available
- Track can break if stepped on
- No reversing available
- No brakes available

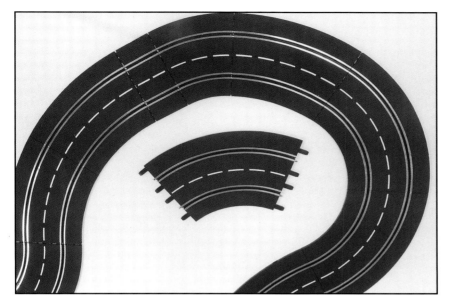

The gap in the track in the previous photo was filled with three small track sections: an outer curve, a 1/4-length straight, and a half-inner curve.

If cars stall on Scalextric or SCX track it may be necessary to gently pry the track rails apart with a screwdriver to restore the proper slot width.

Riggen track is black rather than the gray of Revell track. Riggen offers a standard 60-degree curve and a 30-degree outer curve as well as a standard straight, chicane, and lane crossover track. The lack of a half-length standard curve presents the same problems it does with the Artin track; it's not possible to make 90-degree turns. The Riggen track is better for creating race tracks than Artin's is because the length of the straight and the geometry of the curves allows for the creation of ess bends without the need for half-length or shorter straight sections. A track-planning guide is available with the Riggen track. Four-lane tracks can be constructed with the Riggen system, but at present, no borders of any kind are available. Riggen is available to dealers through R.E.H. Distributors. The track has a tab-and-slot system with snap interlocks. The lane spacing is 3 1/2 inches.

The track originally sold by Strombecker is still available in Bachmann packages. Bachmann sold a series of sets with roughly 1/43-scale cars in the 1980s and the track is still available to dealers through R.E.H. Distributors. Only standard curves and straight track sections are available as well as a chicane and crossover track. No borders are available. The Strombecker/Bachmann track has a tab-and-slot system with an optional small plastic pin to lock the track sections together. The lanes are spaced 3-1/2 inches apart.

Race Track Geometry

Scalextric, SCX, and Ninco tracks use a 45-degree curve standard where it takes 8 sections to make a full circle. Carrera, Artin, Riggen (Revell), and Strombecker/Bachmann use a 30-degree system that takes 12 track sections to make a circle. Unfortunately, Artin, Riggen, and Strombecker/Bachmann only offer double-length standard curves of 60 degrees, which among other difficulties, makes it impossible to create a 90-degree turn.

Scalextric, SCX, Ninco, and Carrera offer the most versatile systems for designing your own tracks or for duplicating the action and design of real race tracks. Scalextric offers the widest choice of unusual track sections, but has no outer-outer curve. The choice of smaller curves allows you to create your own track designs and still have track sections available to fill in the

Use a razor saw to cut Carrera straight borders to fit outside the 1/4 straights and 1/3 straights.

gaps. One of the track design tricks that you can use is a series of tight ess bends that can be assembled from half-length SCX or Scalextric standard curves. The half curves can also be used to create a two-piece ess bend to fill in odd-sized gaps in the track. An unusual but interesting ess bend can be made by connecting two of the crossover tracks end-to-end.

The choice of different curve radii allows you to create increasing and decreasing radius turns. The turn in the photo was made from four pieces of Carrera outer curves and a single standard curve. This is more interesting to see and to race on than just the standard curve, but it requires about six inches more space and can affect track geometry and make it difficult to connect the final two track sections.

If you lay out a track and discover that the ends do not meet as shown in the photo, it is extremely helpful to have a variety of short curved and straight track sections available. I assembled about 20 sections of Carrera track around a ping-pong table, and when it came time to join the ends, the standard curve was not long or large enough to fill this gap, and two outer curves were too big and not long enough. What worked was a combination of an outer curve, a half-standard curve, and a 1/4-length straight. There are no rules or shortcuts to making the track fit; you just need to experiment. In some cases, you may have to relocate half the track to get it all to fit. An option is to simply use a published plan and expand or contract where possible to fit your space by adding matching pairs of straight tracks as shown at the places marked with the LL, WW, XX, and YY on the tracks shown in chapters 7 and 8.

Maintaining the Race Track

All of the brands of 1/32-scale race tracks are rugged enough to require very little maintenance. The track should be dusted with a clean, lint-free cloth before every race. About once a month, use some of

A Fly Lola T70 Mark IIIB and a Porsche 917 scream through an ess bend on a Scalextric track. The inner and outer borders flank a standard curve. The hay bales are from Scalextric's C633 Trackside Safety accessory pack.

the track cleaning fluid sold for model railroads to clean the pickup rails. Eventually, the track surface itself may need to be cleaned. Never clean the track with any solvent that could melt or damage the plastic. Plain soap and water is fine. The rails can be polished with a hard rubber eraser like those sold for cleaning model railroad tracks. It's also a good idea to vacuum the slots occasionally, especially if the track is being operated on the floor.

Troubleshooting Track

It is very unusual for problems to occur that are the track's fault. If only one car has a problem, it's likely to be the fault of the car. If all the cars have problems on just one lane, suspect the controller or its connection to the track. Swap controllers to see if that solves the problem.

If you find that any car slows or jolts at one certain place on the track, suspect too-close rail spacing. The rails on the Scalextric or SCX track can be bent inward due to the flexible nature of the track. The rails can be easily pried apart with a screwdriver. The rails on the other brands of track are spaced with a rigid plastic spacer molded into the track. It is unusual for a problem of a stalled car to be poor electrical contact between the track sections. It is possible to force the Scalextric and SCX track sections together so the individual metal strips on the assembly tabs are bent. If you have a problem with one section of the track being "dead," remove it and check all the joints between its rails and the rails of adjoining tracks to be sure they are bent so they make contact.

The only problems you can expect with Carrera, Artin, Riggen, or Strombecker/Bachmann tracks are that an aligning tab may break if you try to force the track apart while disassembling or if you step on the track. The plastic used in these brands can be repaired with plastic cement. I recommend using five-minute epoxy to repair the track because the epoxy joint should be as strong as the track while the cemented plastic joint will still be weak.

To paint the Carrera (shown) or Artin borders, first spray the border white. For a simple concrete border, mask the edge nearest the track with a single strip of 1/8-inch-wide automobile body masking tape. To create red and white rumble strips, mask off 3/8-inch segments of the white along the track edge of he border with 3/8 inches of the ends of 3/8-inch- wide address labels. Then spray the edge of the border red.

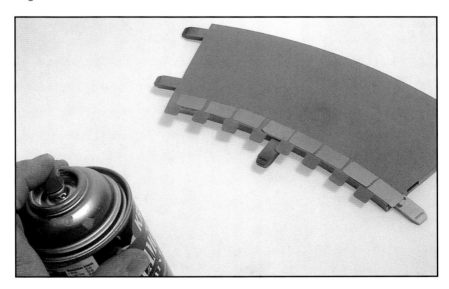

Use more 3/8-inch-wide address labels to mask off the red. Align these labels carefully because they define the inner edge of the rumble strip.

Stow-Away Sectional Track

All of the tracks shown in this book are designed for quick and easy assembly and disassembly. None of the tracks need to be attached permanently to a tabletop except for an HO track where you want to glue down borders to leave room for the cars to slide. That can be avoided by just racing on the two inner lanes or by cutting borders that can be cemented to the sides of the track rather than the table.

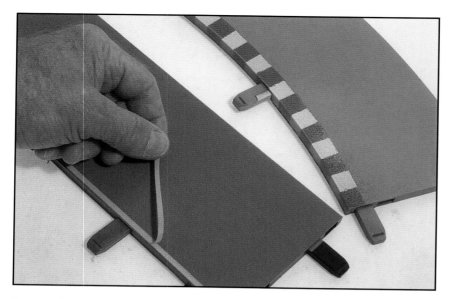

by type in a box, but the majority of Carrera track is stored as these sub-assembled modules.

The Most Important Accessories You Can Buy

The most important accessories you can buy for your 1/32-scale track are the borders (that extend the width of the track so that cars on the outer lanes of every curve can slide out as far as the cars on the inner lanes). I strongly recommend that you fit these borders to the outside of every curve. Borders are also needed on the inside of some curves in the center of an ess bend. You will need borders for at least two full straight track sections connected to any curve because it takes the cars at least two feet to stop power sliding from side to side, or fishtailing as the car accelerates out of the turn.

Remove the masking labels to reveal the red and white rumble strips (top) or pull back the 1/8-inch tape to reveal the concrete border at the edge of the track.

Scalextric, SCX, and Ninco tracks can be disassembled so quickly that it is easiest to snap every section apart and store the track in boxes with stacks of the same-size track to make it easier to find the size you need the next time you assemble a track. If you tilt the track upward one section at a time, the Scalextric and SCX track tabs will almost spring free of their own accord, so you only need flick one or two tabs open with your fingertip. Ninco's tabs hold tight enough that you'll need to flip each of them open to disassemble the track. Almost any track in this book can be assembled in a half-hour once you understand where the track sections belong and have learned the system for assembling the track. The track can be disassembled in even less time.

It takes more time and energy to disassemble or assemble Carrera track. The task isn't difficult, but it is more time consuming, and most joints should be locked with two of Carrera's U-clips. I find that an advantage because the track can be assembled into "modules" such as a 180-degree turn, 4 feet of straight track, or the "Corkscrew." With these modules, I can build new tracks as quickly as I can from scratch with

The labels do not seal tightly enough on the slightly rough track surface, but it is easy enough to touch-up the edges of the paint with white enamel.

Scalextric or SCX track because I only need to assemble about a third of the track from individual sections. The modules are especially time saving when assembling or disassembling four-lane tracks because many of the four-lane curves can be stored as complete four-lane assemblies. I store the pre-assembled modules inside the folded-up ping-pong table that serves to support them during races. I stack the individual sections

Ninco offers borders to fit nearly all of their track sections. Scalextric offers straight borders, but they must be cut to fit the shortest sections. Carrera also offers borders for the straight track sections, but they need to be cut to fit the 1/4 and 1/3 track sections. You can use a razor saw to cut the borders. Plan the cuts carefully so you have at least one attaching tab or one pair of end-to-end tabs on each of the cut sections.

Simple Scenery—The Track Borders

The SCX borders can technically be classified as scenery. They have realistic red and white "rumble" strips, and are green to resemble grass. Unfortunately, the borders are not wide enough to help, but you can use the wider Scalextric borders on everything but the SCX outer-outer curves. Scalextric has realistic curved borders for their standard curves, and they offer a transition border for one straight that also has red and white "rumble" strips. The Scalextric borders are beige to represent the sand traps common on the outside of turns on real race tracks.

In my opinion, the Scalextric straight borders and outer curve borders and the Ninco borders are not realistic enough because both have a garish red and white pattern that is rare on real tracks. The black borders with yellow "Construction Zone" chevrons on the Carrera and Artin tracks are even less realistic. The Carrera, Ninco, and Scalextric borders can be painted, but you may have trouble finding paint that will stick to the flexible plastic.

I painted all of the borders for the 9 x 14-foot Carrera track in chapter 8 in about three hours spaced over three days. Join three or four borders together to protect the assembly tabs, and mask off the tabs on the ends. Begin by spraying the track section white and let that dry overnight. Next, mask off the areas that you want to remain white. I used a single strip of automobile body shop 1/8-inch-wide masking tape to mask off the concrete curbs on some of the borders. I used 3/8-inch labels that were cut in half to mask off the white between the red for the rumble strips. I then sprayed the edge of the track red for the rumble strips and let it dry overnight. Finally, I masked off the red with the same size 3/8-inch-wide labels I used for the white. The final step is to spray the entire track green (I found a flat interior color similar to Sherwin Williams' SW2376 Covent Garden green in a spray can). You could also use the Sherwin Williams color, but the

latex won't stick as well as the enamel from the spray can. I found a sand-colored beige among a series of camouflage colors. When the paint is dry, carefully peel back the masking tape. I painted my tabletop with the Sherwin Williams Covent Garden Green so the borders blend right in.

The double guardrail on the Scalextric Standard curve borders looks the most realistic compared to other brands. I found I could attach the Carrera brackets to the Scalextric guardrails. I also mounted some of the Scalextric guardrails directly to the Carrera borders by drilling 1/8-inch holes to match the spacing of the Scalextric "posts," and then carving the corners square with a hobby knife.

Tables for 1/32-Scale Tracks

A ping-pong table is an ideal off-the-floor support for a 1/32-scale race track. The ping-pong tables are 5 x 9-feet, which is enough space to build some of the best 1/32-scale tracks. There are plans in chapters 7 and 8 for a variety of tracks to fit a 5 x 9-foot space. The table is also strong enough to

Scalextric's newer guardrails can be adapted to a Carrera track by forcing the Scalextric guardrails into the Carrera clips. An alternate method is to drill 1/8-inch holes in the Carrera borders, carve the corners square with a hobby knife, and then push the Scalextric guardrail posts into the holes.

withstand hits from drivers and corner marshals frantically grabbing for deslotted cars during the heat of a race. The table must be placed with the narrow end against the wall or in the middle of the room so the center of the table is easily accessible to grab the deslotted cars.

You can certainly build permanent tables for your race car track. There are also a variety of heavy-duty portable tables with folding legs, including 2-1/2 x 6-foot and 2-1/2 x 8-foot conference tables. The 5 x 9-foot ping-pong tables like this one are often designed so they fold up onto a 2 x 5-foot platform with wheels so they can be rolled away into a closet. You can store the boxes or pre-assembled modules of track between the two tabletops when the table is folded.

If you need to reach more than 3 feet across the track, you'll need to use one of these "reacher" devices.

If you want a larger space to assemble a track, consider using two ping-pong tables side by side to make a 10 x 9-foot space, or end to end to make a 5 x 18-foot space. The 5 x 18-foot space is ideal, especially for four-lane tracks. If you only have room for the 9 x 10-foot two-ping-pong table track, all four sides need to be accessible. There are plans in chapter 8 that require 9 x 12- and 9 x 14-feet of space. You can buy tables for those spaces by using two or even three ping-pong tables side by side or two ping-pong tables plus a 2-1/2 x 8-foot conference table. Major office supply stores, rental yards, and major school supply stores sell the sturdy conference tables at prices as low as $40 for a 6-foot length or $50 for an 8-foot length, or they may be located at flea markets or through classified ads.

Four Scalextric C639 Pit Stop buildings, two sets of their C635 Pit Crews, and one set of their C634 Spectators were used to make this busy pit scene. The McLaren and Jordan are Scalextric cars, and the Ferrari, a 1999 from Pro-Slot, and a Scalextric Williams.

Close up, the pit activity has all the action of real racing pits. MRRC and Preiser also offer mechanics and construction workers that can be used to create pit scenes.

They are sturdy enough for model car racing. Five conference tables are required for the 9 x 12-foot tracks. You could also use two 5 x 9-foot ping-pong tables and a single conference table.

My 9 x 12 track is assembled on two 6 x 6-foot lightweight tabletops plus a 3 x 6-foot tabletop, all made from laminating two layers of 1/2-inch Gatorfoam and covering the edges with 1-inch extruded plastic channels. These materials are available from firms that sell supplies for building portable displays for trade shows. I support the 6 x 6-foot tabletops with a single ping-pong table in the center and folding steel sawhorses on the extreme ends.

Reaching the Unreachable

If you possibly can, arrange your tables so you can walk completely around them for access to deslotted cars. If you can do that, you can have tracks as wide as 6 feet and as

long as you wish; 12, 18, or 24 feet long. I had to squeeze a 9 x 14-foot tabletop into my only available space, so two of the sides are against walls. I solved the problem by including a 2 x 2-foot access opening in the center of each of my two 6 x 6-foot tabletops. During serious race meetings, a corner marshal sits on a stool in each of the two access openings. When I'm racing alone or with just two or three friends, we use a device to pick up hard-to-reach items: larger drug stores and medical supply stores offer a variety of different "reachers." Some have fairly hard tips that can damage the cars. I found a reacher with rubber suction cups soft enough to grip cars as gently as your fingertips. I did bend the tongs and the spring so the reacher could extend out wide enough to grab the front and rear of the car, rather than just the sides.

Remember, race tracks can be built on the floor if you'd rather

not invest in tables. The advantage of the ping-pong and conference tables is that they are portable. The whole 9 x 12-foot tabletop and table folds into the 2 x 5-foot floor space occupied by the folded-up ping-pong table, including space for boxes of track or pre-assembled track sections.

Race Track Realism

If you assemble your track on a permanent tabletop, there's no limit to how realistic you can make the track. Some modelers screw the track to the tabletop, but I do not recommend it. If you lock yourself into a single track, you're missing much of the fun that comes from racing on different tracks without ever leaving your own home. If you feel the track must be fastened to the tabletop, use a latex-based caulking cement such as Liquid Nail's Projects and Foam Board cement or Chem Rex PL300 Foam

Preiser offers a wide selection of both seated and standing spectators, each painted with precision. Preiser also offers a range of unpainted figures.

Board Adhesive. Position the track exactly where you want it and race on it for at least a month to be certain you don't want to change it before cementing the track in place. You can then attach the track to the tabletop with a thick bead of caulking cement down the outside edges of the track. If you do want to move the track later, run a steel spatula between the tabletop and the track to slice through the cement and free the track sections.

The wire screen and plaster techniques common with model railroads or the similar paper towels dipped in Hydrocal plaster can be used to shape mountains and valleys around the track. Do not use loose textures such as ground foam sold for model railroad scenery or sawdust around a race track. If you want surface textures, mix some anti-skid texture compound with latex paint and paint the scenery.

A suggestion: consider making the scenery as portable as the track. If the borders are painted, there won't be much space left for scenery, but the tabletop can be

MRRC has five different assortments of 1/32-scale figures including drivers, pit crew, spectators, and press people. The figures are only available in unpainted sets.

painted to match the green on the borders. For a realistic texture, drape the tabletop with green felt to simulate tracks in the greener parts of the world, or beige felt to re-create the atmosphere of the tracks in arid regions. Avoid any loose textures for

trees or bushes. Trees with flexible trunks and clumps of green lichen moss are available from model railroad shops. Eighteen packages of Life-Like's 1971 Super Giant Oak Trees were used to create the 9 x 12-foot tabletop layouts in this book.

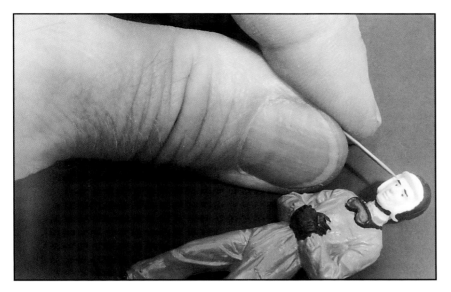

Use a toothpick to apply the tiny details like eye colors, eyebrows, and buttons to the figures. This is one of the MRRC figures.

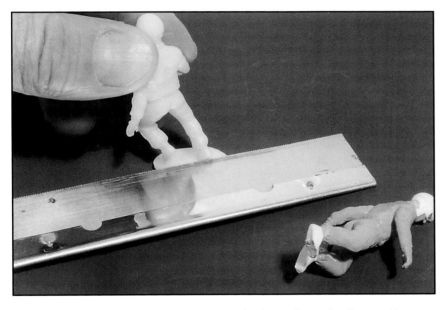

For more realism, use a razor saw to cut the bases from the figures. You can then hold them to the track with pins or rubber cement.

Scalextric also offers a classic Goodyear tire spectator foot bridge. A pit wall made of white Lego blocks can be painted a light concrete gray.

Scalextric has three series of painted pit crew, driver, and spectator figures that are somewhat toylike. MRRC offers five series of figures from the original Airfix and Monogram tooling that are superbly detailed, but you must paint them yourself. Some of these figures are visible in the racing pit scenes in this book. The MRRC assortments include race drivers, pit crew, track officials, spectators, and vendor and reporter figures. Preiser also offers superbly detailed unpainted figures including workmen and both sitting and standing spectators. Preiser also offers painted and detailed 1/32-scale figures. I used the 63054, 63061, and 63074 seated figures, and the 63069 standing figures in the Scalextric grandstand and pit areas.

The Scalextric figures and some of the MRRC have large bases so they are free-standing. However, the bases impart a toylike appearance. You can remove the bases with a razor saw. Drill a hole up through the foot of the figure using a No. 76-size drill bit, insert a common straight pin with the head cut off, and press the figures into Gatorfoam tabletops. You can also drill a No. 76-size hole in the skid aprons on the platforms or stairs of the buildings so the figures can be plugged into the holes. An alternate method is to simply attach the figure's feet to the skid aprons or platforms with rubber cement from a stationery store.

The rugged plastic track and the movable accessories allow you to build and rebuild your race track. The track can be assembled on a tabletop, complete with scenery, for a weekend of racing, and then stored away until the next race. It is certainly more fun if the track is ready to race whenever the mood strikes, but you don't have to devote a permanent space for any of these tracks.

Bring Life to Your Raceway

Scalextric and MRRC offer a variety of 1/32-scale pit buildings, control towers, press boxes, and grandstands. The Scalextric buildings are pre-colored and snap together, while the MRRC buildings (ex-Airfix) must be cemented together then painted. R.E.H. has a nice Riggen "Pit Garage" that is simulated white concrete block with green doors, stairs, and roof railings. The upper story from the Scalextric Control Tower is shown resting on the Pit Garage in some of the photos. Artin has a grandstand with unpainted spectator figures that is very similar to the Scalextric grandstand.

7 BUILDING 1/32-SCALE RACEWAYS

Race track designs can be as much a part of the hobby as acquiring the race cars because race track design is virtually a hobby within the hobby. Before you design your own track, assemble at least a half-dozen tracks from existing designs. Your first race car set should include two or three alternative plans that can be assembled with just the track included in the set.

Scalextric and Ninco have track-expander packs that include a selection of track pieces and track plans you can create by adding sections to the basic figure-8 set of track. Scalextric offers a book of track plans called *31 Track Plans*. Ninco has a CD with track plans called *Track Map*, and Carrera has a track plan *Circuit Planner* CD. If you remember three things from this book, make sure one of them is to buy at least one of these track plan aids so you can see how wild 1/32-scale tracks can be. Also remember to make borders or skid-aprons your second purchase, and larger-radius curves your third purchase.

The Best Tracks for Racing

The track design or track should never be the cause of a crash or spinout. If that sounds ridiculous,

A Fly Porsche 917 and Ferrari 512M sweep through the ess bends on the Ascari 5 x 9-foot track. This track was assembled from Scalextric track sections. The grandstands, control tower, and pit buildings are also Scalextric, and the trees are Life-Like products.

This Neubauer track can be assembled with the sections in the popular Scalextric Formula One set, Le Mans 24 hr set, or a basic oval set plus Scalextric's Track Extension Pack C. Borders have been added to all the curves and on the ends of the straights to supplement those included in the sets and expander packs. The track fits a 5 x 9-foot space.

consider exactly what causes cars to crash on the track. In many cases, it's because they fall off the edge. That problem can be solved with guardrails, but guardrails don't allow the cars to slide. A better solution is to increase the width of the track. Virtually every manufacturer of 1/32-scale tracks offers track edge extenders that may be called borders, skid aprons, side tracks, or other terms. Most firms also offer guardrails that can be attached to the skid aprons to keep the cars from sliding completely off the track or table.

Race-Designed Tracks

It may seem obvious that a race track is designed for racing, but it's not that simple. Just because the track is assembled correctly does not mean the track is going to be fun to race on. Fun can come in several forms, including the "Point-And-Shoot" design for a 1/32 track, or the "In-The-Corners-Action" design.

Whichever track design you choose, even if it's a combination of the two, there will have to be

some compromises. The first is the track itself and the fact that there is only a limited choice of radii. The second limitation is space. The third limitation is how well the cars can be seen. In my opinion, the track must be designed so the cars are never more than about 10 to 12 feet away from any driver or you won't be able to see the car well enough to know whether or not the powerslide is under control. Other model car racers feel that 20 feet is close enough. If space is not a problem, experiment to determine the most comfortable size track for you. It is your track and only you need to be pleased with it.

Borders for Powersliding Cars

By adding borders to all the curves, you make it possible to have as much fun sliding around the outer as the inner lane. You will also need to add borders roughly a foot down the straight so the cars have room to straighten from their tail-out powerslide as they accelerate down the straight away. In tight ess curves, you may also need borders

on the inside of the track to give the cars room to tuck their tails back in from a right-hand powerslide to a left-hand powerslide. Generally, the inside borders are more for appearance than to improve racing action. You'll know where you need more borders because the car will literally fall off the edge of the plastic track.

If you build a four-lane track, nothing should stop you from using the inner two lanes so that the outer two lanes effectively become borders or skid apron areas. If you prefer the non-skid racing performance of cars with strong magnets and sometimes run a few cars without magnets, the inside lanes can be used for races with cars that do have magnets.

Figure-8 Overpasses

A theory among some model car racers is that the length of each lane must be equal to provide equal racing. In reality, there are many factors that influence how fast each lane may be compared to the other lanes. Frankly, it's almost impossible to make all lanes equal, and the solution is simple enough; each driver must spend an equal time on each lane. If you want to try equalizing the lane lengths, it can be done by creating a figure-8 track with an overpass. SCX and Carrera have special bridge tracks to make the transition from flat to upgrade and back down again as smooth as possible. Other manufacturers simply provide elevating supports, and the transitions are accomplished mostly at the track joints. You can bend the track sections vertically to produce smoother bottom-of-the-hill and top-of-the-hill transitions much like those on Carrera's 29545 Crossing track sections.

The race car sets usually tell you where to install track supports. There is a simple system to installing track supports. Start by installing supports that are tall enough to clear the track below. Usually 3 to 4 inches is enough to allow you to fit your hand beneath the bridge to reach a deslotted car. Install just the supports

Key to the 1/32-Scale Carrera or Artin/Track Required

Each of the track plans in this book has letters on the track sections so you can identify what sections are required. This chart will help determine which pieces are used. Carrera numbers their curves with a No. 1 for the inner curve, a 2 for the middle curve, and a 3 for the outer curve. Carrera's banked curves occupy the same table space and are assigned the same 1, 2, and 3 size numbers.

Key to the 1/32-Scale Carrera or Artin Track Required

Key Part No.	Description Part No.	Carrera Part No.	Border Part No.	Artin	Artin Border
H	1/2 Inner Curves	20577	20567	none	none
S	Inner Curves	20571	20561	5712	in set*
K	Banked Inner Curves	20574	20564	5714	in set*
O	Middle Curves	20572	20562	5718	in set*
M	Banked Middle Curves	20576	20565	none	none
OO	Outer Curves	20573	20563	none	none
N	Banked Outer Curves	20575	20566	none	none
E	1/4 Straight	20612	none	none	none
D	1/3 Straight	20611	none	none	none
B	Full Straight	20509	20560	5711	none
Q	Overpass Bridge (Crossing)	20545	none	none	none
R	1/2 of Overpass Bridge	20545	none	none	none
A	Connector	20515	20560	in set	none

(Good location for plug-in controller track. Replace one standard straight, above.)

C	Chicane (lane-narrowing) Track	20516	20560	5717	none

(Good location for chicane. Replace two standard straights, above.)

L	Track can be expanded in length by adding matched pairs of straight track sections here.
T	Turn numbers (correspond to real race course).
W	Track can be expanded in width by adding matched pairs of straight track sections here.
X	Track can be expanded diagonally here by adding matched pairs of equal-length straight track sections.
Y	Track can be expanded diagonally here by adding matched pairs of equal-length straight track sections.

Artin Note: Artin utilizes the same 30-degree-curve geometry as Carrera, so some of these plans can be adapted to use a Carrera track, but a slightly smaller space will be required. Artin does not offer 1/2-inner curve sections, so you must use outer curves any place where a half-curve is required. Also, Artin does not offer any 1/2-, 1/3- or 1/4-length straight track sections, so some of these plans may not align properly unless special track sections are cut to fit.

*NOTE: Artin does not offer borders as accessory items; they are included in most sets. Borders for two-lane "standard" curves are only available with two-lane sets. Curves for outer borders are only available in four-lane sets.

---

that are needed at the edges of the lower track to maintain the minimum 3- to 4-inch separation. You'll now have rather twisted track with very abrupt changes from flat to uphill to equally abrupt changes at the top of the hill. The purpose of the remaining track supports is to minimize the transitions. I usually install the

"second" set of track supports at the places where the track is touching the table at either end of the up- and downhill section. I make these supports about half the height of the tallest supports beside the overpass. That's usually enough to smooth out those vertical transitions from tabletop to upgrade and back down again.

Finally, additional supports are added so there are at least two supports for each track section; one on either side of the track. In some cases, the track supports can be mounted on the borders, and in other cases supports are needed for the borders and track.

The relatively flexible Scalextric and SCX tracks are particularly difficult to support, especially if the borders are attached. Do not hesitate to use duct tape stuck beneath the track to help supplement the weak clips that hold the Scalextric, SCX, and Ninco borders to the track. The borders on these brands hold well enough for a tabletop, but when the track is elevated or operated on a thick carpet, the borders often become loose due to the rumble of passing race cars.

The secret to installing the supports for the crossing bridges is to be sure that each support actually touches the track at the bottom and that it supports the track. If you can push down on the track and it moves 1/16 inch or more, that's the place to install the next-tallest support. Check the track at each support to be sure the track does not move downward where

This Hawthorn Track fits in the same 5 x 9-foot space as the Neubauer Track and uses almost the same number of track sections, but it has no overpass. The Hawthorn is more fun to drive than the Neubauer track because the figure-8-style overpass blocks the sight of the cars at a critical part of the track.

Key to the 1/32-Scale Scalextric, SCX or Ninco Track Required

Key Part No.	Description Part No.	Scalextric Border	SCX Border	Scalextric	SCX
U	1/2 Inner Curve	C152	84010	none	78940
Z	Inner Curve	C156	none	C906	none
H	1/2 Standard Curve	C154	(see Scalextric)	none	none
S	Standard Curve	C151	84000	C8037	87930
O	Outer Curve	C153	84020	C907	87950
OO	Outer-outer Curve	see SCX	84030	see SCX	87960
E	1/4 Straight	C158	84040	none	none
D	1/2 Straight	C159	84050	C186	none
B	Full Straight	C160	84060	C186	87920
A	Connector	C8014	84240	C186	87920

(Good location for plug-in controller track. Replace one standard straight, above.)

C	Chicane (lane-narrowing) Track	C8031	84180	C186	87920

(Good location for chicane. Replace two standard straights, above.)

L   Track can be expanded in length by adding matched pairs of straight track sections here.
T   Turn numbers (correspond to real race course).
W   Track can be expanded in width by adding matched pairs of straight track sections here.
X   Track can be expanded diagonally by adding matched pairs of equal-length straight track sections.
Y   Track can be expanded diagonally by adding matched pairs of equal-length straight track sections.

Ninco Note: Ninco utilizes the same 45-degree-curve geometry and straight track length as Scalextric and SCX, so most of these plans can be adapted to use Ninco track, but a slightly larger space will be required. Some 1/2-straight sections may be needed to maintain track alignment. Ninco does not offer a half-inner curve or a half-standard curve, but none of the plans in this book require either of those sizes.

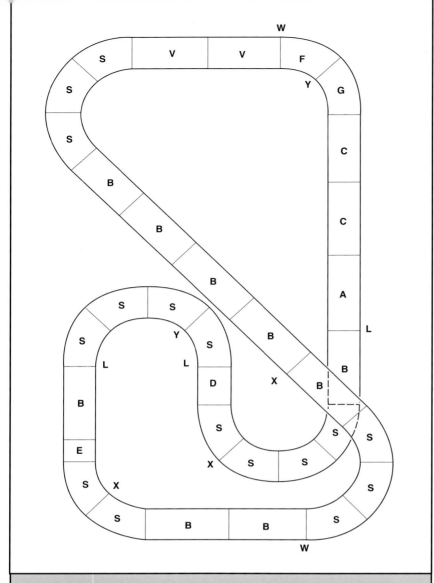

you apply pressure with your hand. For really long overpasses over a four- or six-lane track or overpasses on a curve, you may need to buy additional track supports.

Crossover Tracks

The second method of equalizing the actual length of each lane is to install crossovers–tracks that merely swap lanes. All of the manufacturers supply crossovers. They provide a place on the track where cars cannot pass, but they do give the effect that one car is moving over to pass another. I have connected two crossings back-to-back on some of the tracks to produce a series of short ess-curves or "wiggles." Where two cars enter one of these crossings, it looks like the second car is attempting to pass and is being blocked by the first car. It's an interesting and realistic effect.

Chicanes and Squeeze-Tracks

All of the manufacturers offer track sections that squeeze the two lanes so close together that two cars cannot pass. The term "chicane" was used to describe the abrupt turns that have been added to many full-size race tracks along the straight-away to reduce the length of the straight and lower speeds. On a model car track the chicane serves to provide a place where cars cannot pass, just as there are places on a real track where they cannot pass.

Banked Curves

Carrera offers three different sizes of banked turns. A two-, four-, or six-lane track with banks can be constructed, as shown in chapter 8. Artin offers a standard banked curve as a 30-degree section. Scalextric also offers a standard banked curve, but the bank and radius combined are too severe to allow anything but older cars and some classic cars to negotiate the corners. Some low and long modern cars may also have trouble negotiating the Artin banked turns, and some may have trouble on the standard (No. 1-size) Carrera banked turn.

When assembling a four-lane banked turn, the outer bank track's edges are nearly a foot off the table, and the outer edges of the outer-outer banked curve of a six-lane track are even higher. It is extremely important to have at least two straight track sections, or two curved track sections curving in the same direction as the banked curve, between the bank and level portion of the track. If you are building a four-lane bank, you really need four straight sections, and with a six-lane bank, you should really allow six straight track sections to give the track room to mesh. Remember, the four-lane bank begins at the outside of the inner curve, which means its base height begins at the top of the elevation of the inner-banked curve. Similarly, the height of the inner edge of the outer-outer curve for a six-lane bank begins at the top of the middle-banked curve. The track from the middle- and outer-banked turns must have enough room to straighten out to flat and come downhill.

The Corkscrew Turn

One of the most photographed turns in the world is turn 6 at the Laguna Seca road course near Monterey, California. Turn 6 is a left-hander that drops downhill from the highest straight away on the track, through a tight right-hander at turn 6a, through a slightly curved straight, and into a broader left-hander at turn 7. The track drops 160 feet from the top of turn 6 to the apex of turn 7 in 846 feet of race track and most of that "drop" takes place through turns 6 and 6a. It's one of the most famous tracks in the world, in part because Alex Zanardi used the grass to make a last lap pass to win the 1999 CART open-wheeled car race.

It is difficult to create a 1/32-scale version of the ess-bends at the Corkscrew because the standard flat-curved sections produce an off-camber effect as shown in chapter 8. Even with the flexible Scalextric and SCX track, the off-camber cannot be avoided. It is possible to re-create turns 6 and 6a in 1/32 scale with a Carrera track because they offer the combination of banked turns that work effectively. The Corkscrew turn is part of the Ascari track in this chapter, and it is included on the two Carrera versions of the Paramount Ranch Track in chapter 8.

Compare the 5 x 9-foot Carrera tracks in this chapter to see

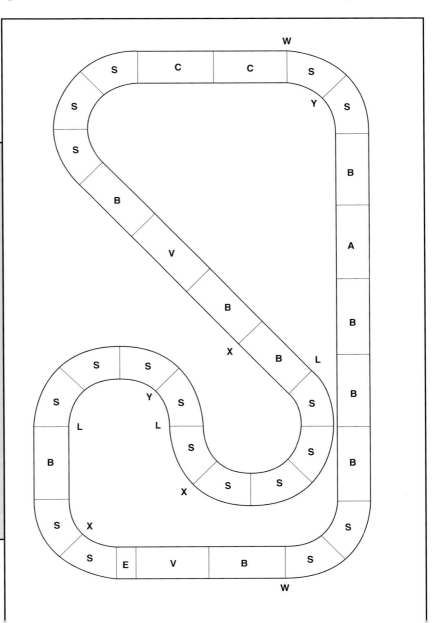

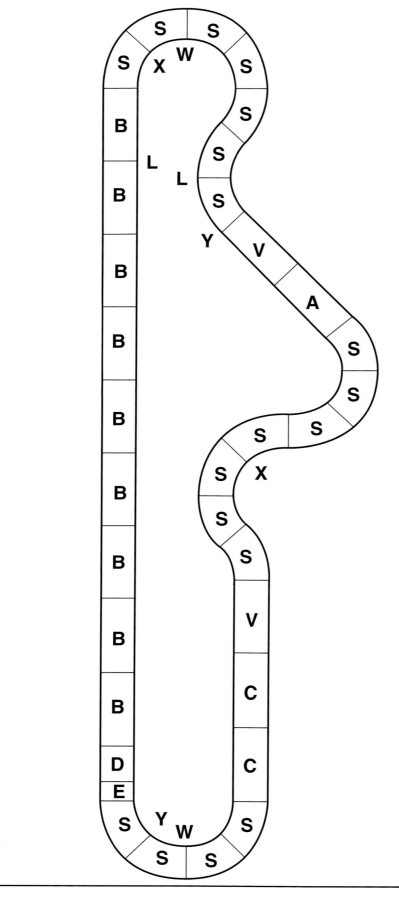

Right

The 4-1/2 x 14-foot Brescia Track utilizes nearly all of the same track pieces as the Neubauer or Hawthorn Tracks, but has been designed to allow the longest possible length of straight.

the difference between a standard flat curve and the Corkscrew. The turn begins with one-half of Carrera's 20545 "Crossing" overpass bridge to bring the track uphill. There's a quarter-length straight No. 20612 at the top, and a standard (No. 1 size, in Carrera's terms) 60-degree curve which allows the track to flex downward. Next are two 30-degree 20574 banked curves which force the track into the diving-down appearance of the Laguna Seca Corkscrew. Next is a half-Standard curve (29577) and another full-Stan-

List of Scalextric or SCX Track Required for 4-1/2 x 14-Foot Brescia Track

Key	Quantity	Description
H	0	1/2 Standard Curve
S	18	Standard Curve
O	0	Outer Curve
OO	0	Outer-outer Curve
E	1	1/4 Straight
D	0	1/2 Straight
B	9	Full Straight
V	2	Crossover Track
A	1	Connector Track
C	2	Chicane (lane-narrowing) Track
L		Track can be expanded in length by adding matched pairs of straight track sections here.
T		Turn numbers (correspond to real race course).
W		Track can be expanded in width by adding matched pairs of straight track sections here.
X		Track can be expanded diagonally here by adding matched pairs of equal-length straight track sections.
Y		Track can be expanded diagonally here by adding matched pairs of equal-length straight track sections.

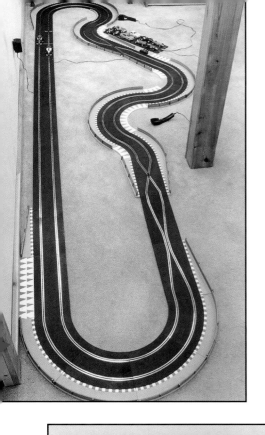

List of Carrera Track Required for 5 x 14-Foot Brescia Track

Key	Quantity	Description
H	0	1/2 Inner Curves
S	10	Inner Curve
K	6	Banked Inner Curve
O	0	Middle Curves
M	0	Banked Middle Curve
OO	0	Outer Curves
N	0	Banked Outer Curve
E	3	1/4 Straight
D	2	1/3 Straight
B	9	Full-Straight
Q	1	Overpass Bridge
R	0	1/2 of Overpass Bridge
A	1	Connector Track
C	2	Chicane
L		Track can be expanded in length by adding matched pairs of straight track sections here.
T		Turn numbers (correspond to real race course).
W		Track can be expanded in width by adding matched pairs of straight track sections here.
X		Track can be expanded diagonally here by adding matched pairs of equal-length straight track sections.
Y		Track can be expanded diagonally here by adding matched pairs of equal-length straight track sections.

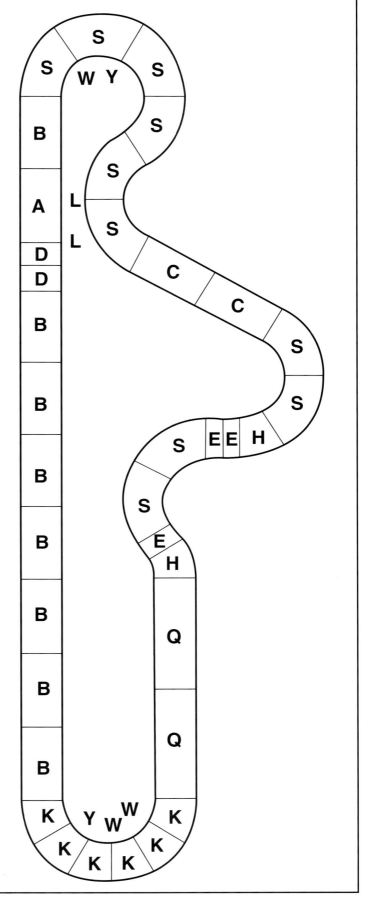

dard curve to bring the track down to level, followed by two No. 3-size outer-outer curves (No. 20573) to provide an increasing-radius turn. On the Paramount Ranch plans in chapter 8, the final curve at the bottom of the corkscrew is a single No. 2-size flat curve (No. 20572) to give the track some length to change from a bank to the flat. A 180-degree curve made from No. 2-size curves continues in the flat. There is a slight off-camber at the bottom of the Corkscrew on the 1/32 Paramount Ranch Track, but it is not enough to affect the car's entrance to that corner.

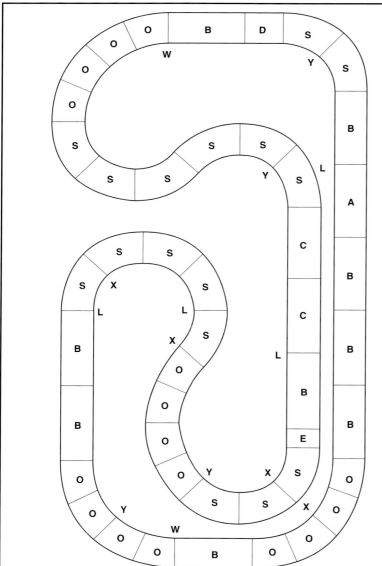

The Ascari Track offers one of the best possible combinations of turns and straights that can be squeezed onto the top of a 5 x 9-foot ping-pong table with Scalextric track.

List of Scalextric or SCX Track Required for 5 x 9-Foot Ascari Track

Key	Quantity	Description
H	0	1/2 Standard Curve
S	18	Standard Curve
O	16	Outer Curve
OO	0	Outer-outer Curve
E	1	1/4 Straight
D	1	1/2 Straight
B	9	Full Straight
V	0	Crossover Track
A	1	Connector Track
C	2	Chicane (lane-narrowing) Track
L		Track can be expanded in length by adding matched pairs of straight track sections here.
T		Turn numbers (correspond to real race course).
W		Track can be expanded in width by adding matched pairs of straight track sections here.
X		Track can be expanded diagonally here by adding matched pairs of equal-length straight track sections.
Y		Track can be expanded diagonally here by adding matched pairs of equal-length straight track sections.

This alternate version of the 5 x 9-foot Ascari track has an SCX outer-outer curve on one end and is banked slightly by adding in an extra couple of inches of straight track in the middle of the curve.

The 1/32-scale Corkscrew track arrangement works spectacularly well on both the 5 x 9-foot and 9 x 12-foot tracks. The 1/32 cars dive down off the hill and dip through turn 6 to sweep around the exit of turn 6a looking just like the cars at Laguna Seca. It's interesting to drive in the uphill opposite direction because it becomes a mini-bank turn that has an effective radius different from any of the available flat sections. There's enough straight so the cars become airborne as they come down the hump in the "Crossing" bridge unless you provide something a bit less

List of Scalextric or SCX Track Required for FOR 5 x 9-Foot "Banked" Ascari Track

Key	Quantity	Description
H	0	1/2 Standard Curve
S	17	Standard Curve
O	8	Outer Curve
OO	8	Outer-outer Curve
E	2	1/4 Straight
D	2	1/2 Straight
B	6	Full Straight
V	0	Connector Track
A	1	Connector Track
C	2	Chicane (lane-narrowing) Track
L		Track can be expanded in length by adding matched pairs of straight track sections here.
T		Turn numbers (correspond to real race course).
W		Track can be expanded in width by adding matched pairs of straight track sections here.
X		Track can be expanded diagonally here by adding matched pairs of equal-length straight track sections.
Y		Track can be expanded diagonally here by adding matched pairs of equal-length straight track sections.

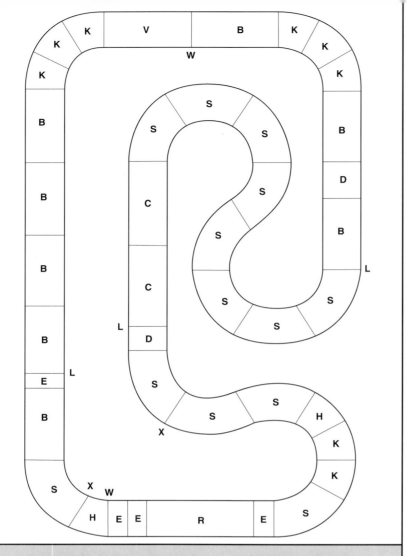

than full-throttle. What's interesting is that the cars with motors in the front leave the track and land back in the slot, while cars with motors in the back often leave the slot for long enough so that they land deslotted. Weight can be added to the rear-motored cars, but there are differences in the handling of real cars and it's nice to have differences in model racers too.

How About an Eight-Lane Track?

Scalextric, SCX, and Ninco offer the option of eight different curve radii so an eight-lane track can be assembled. Frankly, it's not as exciting as it sounds because of the vast difference in the size or radius of the innermost curved lanes compared to the outermost curved lanes. In essence, the outer two lanes are a completely different track from the inner two lanes. For most racers, two lanes are plenty. The four-lane track does offer the advantage of each lane being different with a considerable difference between the "inner" and "outer" lanes, even with a figure-8 design. However, the differences are not so great as to make wheel-to-wheel racing impossible, but four lanes are about the limit before the differences between inside and outside lanes become too great for exciting races. The real advantage to offering four different curve radii is that there are four choices for the sizes of the curves to allow for increasing and decreasing radius turns that make driving a well-designed track more fun.

Carrera offers a choice of six different curve radii because they offer standard, outer, and outer-outer curves as both flat and banked. The banked curves are gentle enough so you can still powerslide most cars around the turn. The banking merely provides a much-larger-radius curve for each track size.

Brake Turns for Point-and-Shoot Track

The inner curves offered by Scalextric, SCX, and Ninco are ridiculously tight so that the car can virtually turn in its length. In the real world of racing and rallying,

turning a car within its length is accomplished by a "brake turn," where the driver applies the emergency brake to lock-up the rear wheels so the car will pivot around the front wheels. Experienced stunt car drivers can brake turn at 60 miles per hour, but it's a trick and not a racing strategy. Frankly, the 1/32-scale cars look very strange cranking around the tight inner turns. The inner turns do allow for an accurate duplication of the shape of a real race track. The inner curves also allow you to add two lanes to some two-lane plans so that a four-lane track can be created, but it will have extremely sharp curves. Those

This version of the 5 x 9-foot Point-and-Shoot Track for Carrera has a flat ess bend in the lower right corner with one of Carrera's outer-outer banked curves sweeping around the back edge of the track.

List of Carrera Track Required for 5 x 9-Foot Point-and-Shoot Banked Track

Key	Quantity	Description
H	4	1/2 Inner Curves
S	13	Inner Curve
K	0	Banked Inner Curve
O	0	Middle Curves
M	0	Banked Middle Curve
OO	0	Outer Curves
N	6	Banked Outer Curve
E	2	1/4 Straight
D	4	1/3 Straight
B	7	Full Straight
Q	0	Overpass Bridge
R	0	1/2 of Overpass Bridge
A	1	Connector Track
C	0	Chicane
L		Track can be expanded in length by adding matched pairs of straight track sections here.
W		Track can be expanded in width by adding matched pairs of straight track sections here.
X		Track can be expanded diagonally here by adding matched pairs of equal-length straight track sections.
Y		Track can be expanded diagonally here by adding matched pairs of equal-length straight track sections.

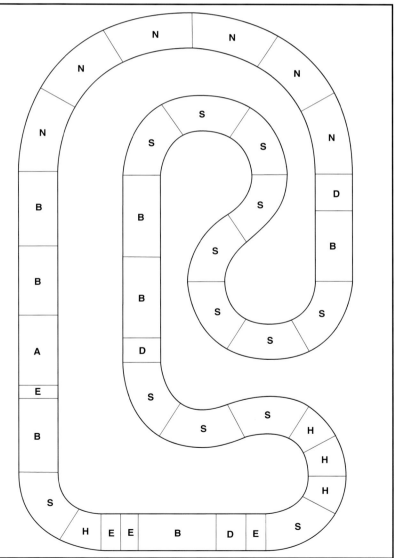

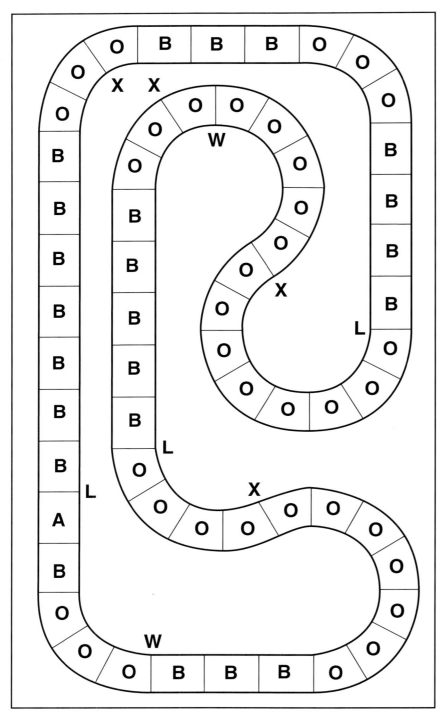

The Point-and-Shoot 6 x 11-foot plan was adapted from an Artin four-lane set. Thirty-six outer curves, twenty straight sections, two chicanes, and a terminal track are required for this track. Two Artin four-lane figure-8 sets plus four more curved track sections (or a third four-lane set) are required to build this track.

ultra-tight inner turns also favor drivers who like the "point-and-shoot" driving technique. I have not included a single inside turn on any track in this book. Since the turns are the smaller inside turns, you can add another two lanes to most of the Scalextric, Ninco (with some modifications to the track design), and SCX tracks.

Two Lanes or Four?

Two racing lanes are plenty for most slot car enthusiasts. In general, a two-lane track looks more realistic because it makes the track look longer. To hold races on a four-lane track, at least eight people are needed: four to drive the cars and at least four to corner marshal. A second inner lane can be added to track plans if the adjacent tracks allow enough room. For example, you could add two inner lanes to the Ascari Raceway plan. In some cases, outer lanes can be easily added. The plans for a 9 x 12-foot and 9 x 14-foot Indy F1 Grand Prix Track for the Paramount Ranch Track are designed to be expanded from two lanes to four.

How Much Track Should I Buy?

Enough of your favorite brand of track should be purchased to build any 1/32-scale track in this book if you have the space. The 9 x 12-foot tracks don't require much more track than the designs for 5 x 9-foot spaces; the track is just strung-out around the space. If you have favorite designs, buy enough track to build them all. Scalextric, SCX, and Ninco sell most of their track in packages of two sections. Carrera packages at least twice that many pieces into their minimum-size package, and in most cases, a minimum 180 degrees of curve (or borders for curves) is included in a single box. However, the larger packages usually result in lower-cost sections. Don't be surprised if you find uses for track you never thought you'd want. As an example, I only needed 90 degrees (half a box) of banked track for the 9 x 12-foot version of the Indy Formula One Grand Prix track shown

The 5 x 9-foot Ascari track is one of the best tracks that can be assembled on a 5 x 9-foot ping-pong table with Carrera track. It has just about everything: a high-speed banked turn, corkscrew turn, ess curves, increasing and decreasing radius turns, and the longest straight you can get in the space (amplified by the extra speed available from the banked turn at the end of the straight).

in chapter 8. I also wanted to include the "corkscrew" turns, which needed two more pieces of banked turn.

Scalextric and Ninco sell special "expander" packages of track that include enough track to build specific circuits when added to a basic figure-8 set. The expander packs are much less expensive than buying the individual track sections alone, but you may get more standard straights than you want, so count the track you think you'll need before opting for an expander pack. It is difficult to locate individual sections of Artin track and is far less expensive to buy a $100 Artin four-lane set for 50 pieces of track than to spend $4 a section and only receive 25 pieces for your investment. The extra four cars, four controllers, and another power pack are "free." Before you decide that Artin is a bargain, read the section on Artin track and see if you can live with the compromises.

If you prefer Scalextric track and enjoy racing NASCAR sedans, consider buying Scalextric's Speedway set to obtain enough standard curves and straights for a tri-oval and adding their Super Speedway set to get outer curves and straights to convert the Speedway into a four-lane tri-oval. It's far less expensive

than buying the track and cars separately, and there are sometimes cars offered in the sets that are not available as separate pieces.

Picking the Best Track Plan

When you're looking for the best track plan or are trying to assemble your own custom design, look for these features:

• As many different curve radii that can be included in the available space.
• No more than one right- and one left-hand corner that are 90 degrees or greater and some that are 180 degrees or slightly greater. Right and left combinations of single curved track sections can be joined to produce four- to eight-section ess curves that are fascinating to drive cars through because you can usually get through running flat out.
• Group all the accessory straight track sections such as chicanes and crossover tracks in one area to get the wiggles over in one place, and leave the real straights for other areas.
• Build a track with the longest straight-away that can fit into the available space and/or the longest straight-away that can be built with the amount of track available at the moment. The optimum length of straight-away can vary considerably depending on the brands of cars used, whether or not the cars have strong magnets, and whether or not the track is wired for electric braking.

A look into the banked turn. The two track sections above the modified Scalextric Aston Martin have two solid white lines; those are the two standard banked turns that make the corkscrew possible by forcing the bank. The modified Ninco Testa Rossa Ferrari is drifting over the hump leading down into the corkscrew. It is a full-length standard curve that has a slight hump twisted into it by the banked turns.

Design Your Own 1/32 Raceway

Race track design is fairly simple with a 1/32-scale track because the sizes of curved tracks available are limited. Thus, a "hairpin" turn can only be as small as the standard radius, and a sweeping curve can only be as large as the outer-outer curve track. All three sizes of curves can be used to create increasing-radius and decreasing-radius turns similar to those on the real track. If at all possible, include elevation changes, especially severe drops like the famous "Corkscrew" at Laguna Seca in California. Both Scalextric and Ninco make inner-inner curves, but they are so tight they're more like brake-turns (where a real car turns by a hard application of the rear hand brake) within the length of the car. For racing, the standard curves are about as tight as most racers want.

Race Track Design Priorities (in order):

- All parts of the track within 36 inches of the edge to easily reach deslotted cars.
- Guardrails around the edges of the skid aprons/borders to keep cars off the floor.
- Skid aprons/borders on the outside of every piece of curved track to provide the option of racing cars without magnets.
- The longest straight possible in the space provided.
- Use larger-diameter curved track sections wherever possible.
- Separate power packs for each lane.
- An uphill and downhill section somewhere on the track.
- Banked curve to "extend" the length of at least one straight.

Test drive the track in both directions. Try to design a race track that is fun to drive in either direction to increase the track's usable life. Conversely, if a track drives well in one direction but awful in the other, changing the track design can ruin the good direction.

Experiment by replacing parts of the track with smaller- or larger-radius curves and try increasing and decreasing radius turns as well as banked turns. Be willing to remove and substitute track sections at least a half-dozen times before settling on that as the "best" combination.

Design for Corner Marshals

If you really want to race, design the track so it can be marshaled. Be realistic about how many people will be racing. If there are only two people, you'll have to take turns putting each other's cars back on the track. If you can get four people together, you have two corner marshals available. Resist the temptation to build a four-lane track just because you have four people available. It's far more fun to race just two cars and have two corner marshals to put them back on the track for you. Remember that the track sections have to be close enough to the edge of the table so the corner marshals can reach them (about 3 feet from the edge of the table), which means you have to be able to reach both sides of a 5-foot-wide ping-pong table. An alternative is to design a tabletop with access holes so the corner marshals can sit on stools during the race. For casual racing, you can reach cars as far as 6 feet from the edge of the table by using a reacher device.

Expanding a Figure-8

Scalextric offers an "Expander Pack C" that includes enough track to expand their basic figure-8 (plus four straight-track sections) into a complex bow tie-shaped track that can also be built with Scalextric's popular "Formula One" and "LeMans 24 hr" sets. The track included in these sets and the figure-8 plus "Expander Pack C" is the track used to make the 5 x 9-foot Neubauer and Hawthorn tracks, and the 4-1/2 x 14-foot Brescia track.

Better Than a Figure-8

The figure-8 track configuration on the fictitious Neubauer track is overrated in producing equal lap times. It's the combination of turns that matters more than simply trying for equal distance. The bridge also blocks your view

A look down onto the corkscrew with the crossing sections of Carrera's bridge placed side-by-side rather than end-to-end. The inner section merely serves as a paddock to park waiting race cars. The crossing provides the necessary uphill to allow the corkscrew's downhill, and it helps force the whole thing into both vertical and horizontal alignment.

of part of the track. I have dubbed the revised track the "Hawthorn." Even without the overpass bridge, half of the ess curve is elevated for both appearance and so that the borders do not interfere with the straight-away. If you are driving from the straight-away side of the track, the elevated curve does not interrupt the view of the cars. I find the Hawthorn track far more enjoyable to drive on than the Neubauer track, it requires almost the same amount of track and fits in the same space.

Finding the Long Straight-Away for Scalextric, SCX, and Ninco

This track is designed to produce the longest possible straight-away with Scalextric's Formula One and LeMans 24 hr sets, or a basic figure-8 set plus Scalextric's Expander Pack C track assortment. The fictitious Brescia track utilizes every standard straight in the box and places the crossover, chicane, and controller tracks along the twisting side. There is enough room for nearly any 1/32-scale car to reach top speed on this straight-away. You could put this track on three 2-1/2 x 8-foot conference tables if you don't want to run it on the floor.

The edge of the corkscrew as a Ninco BMW V12LMR and a SCX Ferrari 330SP race through the turns. Note the slight twist to the standard straight as it leads into the banked sections of the turn.

The 5 x 14 Brescia Track, the Long Straight-Away for Carrera

A "long straight-away" plan can be assembled with Carrera track. There's almost enough track in the large Mille Miglia set, but you'll also need to buy a box containing four 20509 straights, a box of four 20612 1/3 straights, a box of four 20611 1/3 straights, and one 60-degree curve. The 20577 30-degree curves can be purchased in a box of six that will be useful, (as will the 1/4 and 1/3 straights) with other tracks. A 20516 chicane or two more straights are also needed. This plan, as most of the others that require half-length standard curves, will not work with Artin tracks unless you're willing to cut your own Artin track sections.

The 5 x 9 Ascari Raceway for Scalextric, Ninco, and SCX

The fictitious Ascari tracks are developments of the previous tracks in this chapter, but some of the standard curves have been supplemented with some outer curves to produce both increasing- and decreasing-radius turns. The two tracks differ only in that the large curve on the alternate version of the Ascari track is assembled for SCX outer-outer curves. You'll find a photo of the track in chapter 1. This is one of the most enjoyable tracks that can be built for Scalextric or SCX in 5 x 9 feet. It would take another 6 inches of length and width to assemble the track with Ninco track sections.

The Ascari track with outer-outer curves is almost identical to the Ascari track with 90-degree outer curves on the end closest to the camera (see photo on page 64). The SCX outer-outer curves fit best on this particular track if the short straight "E" is a Scalextric C157 Short Straight, but the slightly longer C158 1/4 straight will work just fine. I discovered that I could force a gentle bank into the SCX outer-outer curve on this track by substituting a 1/2 straight in the middle of this broad curve. That's how the banking that appears in the photo on page 65 was created.

There are pros and cons involved in replacing outer curves with broader outer-outer curves. Only SCX makes borders for the outer-outer curves, and the borders are really not wide enough to allow a car to powerslide around the corner. With the outer-outer curves, there's the choice of trying to control the slide along the outer lane, or letting the car ride the guardrail. If you are running cars like Fly or MRRC that have very strong magnets, the cars may not slide around this broad curve anyway. Cars with strong magnets can be driven around most of the track at full throttle, and let off for the tight and

abrupt changes in direction. I was able to drive a Fly Panoz LMP Spyder with its strong stock magnets around this track in about 6.1 seconds, and a Ninco Testa Rossa Ferrari without magnets in about 7 seconds. The lap length is about 36 feet.

"Point-And-Shoot" Tracks for Carrera

The 5 x 9-foot "point-and-shoot" track is built with only Carrera inner No. 1-size curves. Some of those curves can be standard-size banked curves included in some Carrera No. 1-size starter sets. It looks like a track for go-karts and drives like one because the throttle is slammed on to accelerate out of corners and flicked off so the brakes will help slide the car into the next corner. Obviously, the sweeping ess bends must be driven at a more-or-less steady throttle, but the entry and exit utilizes the same "point-and-shoot" driving technique. This track includes the "Corkscrew" that can be built with track from some of Carrera's starter sets.

The same track can be built with Scalextric, SCX, or Artin track, but there are already two 5 x 9-foot tracks in this chapter that utilize the standard curves. Conversely, a Carrera track could probably be adapted to either of these configurations, but the "point-and-shoot" track is far more fun to drive. It requires a bit more track, but it's worth it. It also defies one of the "rules" I've provided by not using a variety of curve sizes.

The second "point-and-shoot" track is a variation on the first plan. The Corkscrew is replaced with all No. 1-size flat curves, but the banked turns on the end are replaced with a single sweeping banked turn made from Carrera's unique No. 3-size outer-outerbanked turns. It's an example of how segments of the track can be changed to completely alter the driving patterns. The banked Carrera turns are somewhat more flexible than the same-size flat curves. The track is best aligned if some 1/4 straight track sections are inserted on both the long straight leading into the bank and the short straight across the bottom of the track. The plan

List of Carrera Track Required for 5 x 9-Foot Ascari Track

Key	Quantity	Description
H	3	1/2 Inner Curves
S	9	Inner Curve
K	2	Banked Inner Curve
O	5	Middle Curves
M	0	Banked Middle Curve
OO	2	Outer Curves
N	6	Banked Outer Curve
E	5	1/4 Straight
D	1	1/3 Straight
B	5	Full Straight
Q	0	Overpass Bridge
R	1	1/2 of Overpass Bridge
A	1	Connector Track
C	0	Chicane
L		Track can be expanded in length by adding matched pairs of straight track sections here.
T		Turn numbers (correspond to real race course).
W		Track can be expanded in width by adding matched pairs of straight track sections here.
X		Track can be expanded diagonally here by adding matched pairs of equal-length straight track sections.
Y		Track can be expanded diagonally here by adding matched pairs of equal-length straight track sections.

shows three 1/4 sections, one half-section, and one full-length straight. The sections could be replaced with two full-length straights and a 1/4 straight, but the smaller sections make it easier to align the track and provide the option of fitting the corkscrew sections without changing as much track.

The 6 x 11 Ascari Raceway for Artin

It's not possible to duplicate the complex tracks for Scalextric and SCX track with Artin track because Artin does not offer a half-length standard curve. However, this track can be built in a 6 x 11-foot space by using only the Artin outer curves. The outer curves all come with borders or skid aprons so the cars can powerslide in every corner. The track is not as fun to drive as the Ascari tracks for Scalextric/SCX/Ninco and Carrera because there are only two different lane radii.

The 5 x 9 Ascari Raceway for Carrera

The fictitious Ascari track is one of the most interesting tracks you can build with Carrera track in just 5 x 9 feet. This looks like the "Point-and Shoot" track, but there are three major differences: the curves on the inner ess bends have been revised with outer and outer-sections to replace standard sections to create increasing and decreasing radius turns; the hairpin turn near the short straight has been revised to include the "Corkscrew" turn described earlier in this chapter; and the two banked standard-size curves have been replaced with a broad, sweeping No. 3-size outer banked turn—the fastest turn available for 1/32 scale. This track incorporates just about everything that is fun to drive on a 1/32-scale race track, and it does it in two lanes with a lap length of about 34 feet.

8 REAL 1/32-SCALE RACE TRACKS

Two Carrera 1/32-scale Vipers drift around the sharp turn 1 on the 5 x 9-foot Scalextric version of the Indy F1 Grand Prix Track.

Virtually all the thrill of real racing is captured by assembling a careful recreation of the shape of the real track. It's fairly simple to do with 1/32-scale track because there are a limited number of available sizes of curved tracks. I have deliberately avoided the use of the same-size curves for any of the road racing courses, so all of the Indy F1 Grand Prix and Paramount Ranch track designs have that "In-The-Corners-Action" where each corner is a challenge to be learned and mastered.

The model cars are exact scale replicas of real race cars, so why not model the actual tracks where those cars raced? It sounds like a great idea, but the reality is not what you might expect. If a real race track is reduced to 1/32 scale, the turns will be so large that the cars will never come off the track. With stock gearing, a 1/32-scale race car hits top speed in about 6 to 10 feet. For example, the straight-away on a true-scale 1/32 version of the Indianapolis 500 track would be 100 feet long, so a 1/32-scale car would just grind away at top speed for about 90 feet. Not too exciting.

Indy F1 U. S. Grand Prix Track

The Indianapolis Formula One track snakes around inside the 2.6-mile oval used for the Indianapolis

73

Four Scalextric NASCAR sedans power around a four-lane banked turn on the Scalextric "Indianapolis 500" track.

500 IRL open-wheel race and NASCAR Brickyard 400 race. The Formula One track was built in time for the inaugural Indianapolis Formula One Grand Prix in 2000. Most of the drivers liked the track except for the very tight right and left ess bend in turns 6 and 7, dubbed "Mickey and Minnie." The track allows for extremely high speeds, thanks to the long straight and the banked right-hand turn 13. The F1 cars run the track clockwise, while the IRL and NASCAR cars run counterclockwise, so turn 13 for the F1 cars is turn 1 for the IRL and NASCAR cars.

Indy F1 U.S. Grand Prix Track 5 x 9 for Scalextric and SCX

The plans for 1/32-scale tracks are examples that have the most important features of a real track in an absolute minimum amount of space. The Scalextric and SCX version utilizes the SCX outer-outer curves as a mirror image of the Ascari plan in chapter 7.

Indy F1 U.S. Grand Prix Track 5 x 9 for Carrera

The Carrera version of the Indy F1 track uses Carrera's No. 3-size outer-outercurves for adjoining turns 12 and 13 and allows maximum speed through the corner. Cars cannot be driven through flatout, but it's an incredible sight to watch a car actually powerslide around the banking. I assembled the track with a 180-degree bank, but it's even more fun to race on if you use the flat No. 3-size outer-outer curves for the last 90 degrees to better simulate the flat turn 12 on the real track. Also included is the "Corkscrew" from chapter 7 just because it's such a delight to drive. At the actual Indy you'll find little elevation change, so to be more authentic, you can make this turn flat. However, the downhill sweep effectivley provides a different set of curve radii, so I'd suggest building the corkscrew version for that reason alone. This track is also a mirror-image version of the Ascari plan in Chapter 7.

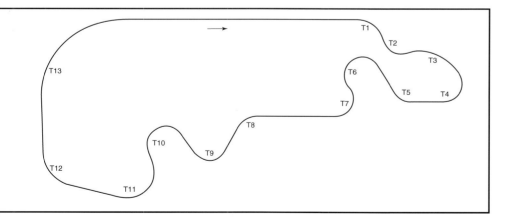

A schematic diagram of the Indy 500 Formula One Grand Prix Track. The cars race in a clockwise direction for this event as opposed to the counterclockwise direction used by the IRL open-wheeled cars and NASCAR sedans. The letter "T" indicates the turn numbers.

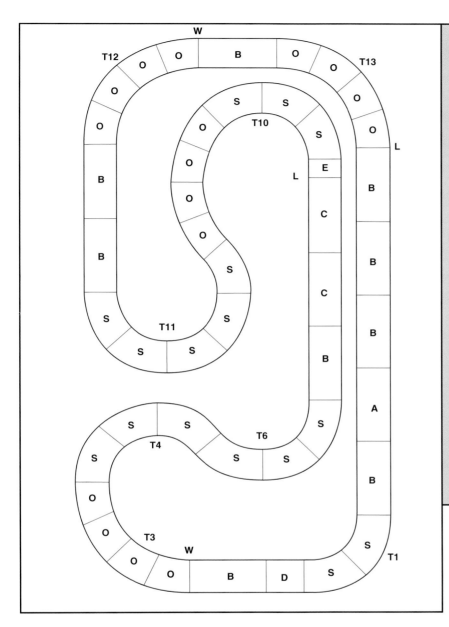

13 is banked for 90 degrees just like the real turn 13, and the relative size of the curves matches those of the prototype track. This track is also designed to allow for the addition of two more lanes inside the existing plan.

Indy F1 U.S. Grand Prix Track 9 x 12 for Scalextric and SCX

It is possible to capture the general shape of the Indy Formula One track with either Scalextric, SCX, or Carrera track. A much more credible track can be built if you have a bit more space. This plan is designed to accept an additional two lanes on the inside of all the curves and the minimum-size curve will be a "standard." None of the too-tight Scalextric or SCX inner curves will be needed. You should be able to build the same track with Ninco using a few different sizes of short straight-track sections, but in an extra foot of space in both directions.

Indy F1 U.S. Grand Prix Track 9 x 12 for Carrera

The Carrera track does not allow a chance to capture all the different turns of the vast Indy Formula One track in a small space. It looks about as much like the real track as the Scalextric/SCX/Ninco version, but it's the corners and the combination of corners and straight-aways that make it like the real track. For instance, turn

Indy F1 U.S. Grand Prix Track 9 x 14 for Carrera

This is the same plan as the 9 x 12-foot Carrera Indy Formula One Grand Prix Track, but the straightaway has been increased by two track sections. This makes a difference for two reasons: it makes the shape of the track more strung-out like the real track, and that extra 2 feet of straight is just enough so that nearly all of the 1/32-scale cars will just reach their top speed before you need to apply the brakes. This version takes 2 more feet of length, so it will require 9 x 14 feet of space.

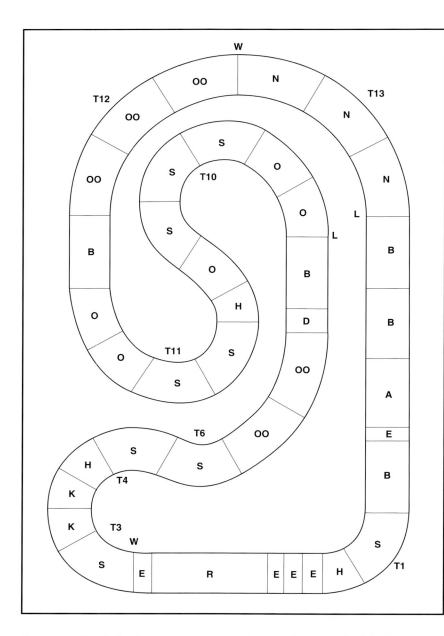

List of Carrera Track Required for 5 x 9-Foot Indy F1 Grand Prix Track
(A list of the part numbers for the track sections and their borders that are identified by the "Key" letters on this plan is shown in chapter 7.)

Key	Quantity	Description
H	3	1/2 Inner Curves
S	9	Inner Curve
K	2	Banked Inner Curve
O	5	Middle Curves
M	0	Banked Middle Curve
OO	3	Outer Curves
N	3	Banked Outer Curve
E	5	1/4 Straight
D	1	1/3 Straight
B	5	Full Straight
Q	0	Overpass Bridge
R	1	1/2 of Overpass Bridge
A	1	Connector Track
C	0	Chicane
L		Track can be expanded in length by adding matched pairs of straight track sections here.
T		Turn numbers (correspond to real race course).
W		Track can be expanded in width by adding matched pairs of straight track sections here.
X		Track can be expanded diagonally here by adding matched pairs of equal-length straight track sections.
Y		Track can be expanded diagonally here by adding matched pairs of equal-length straight track sections.

Paramount Ranch Track

The Paramount Ranch Track is certainly one of the most obscure tracks on the planet. It only operated for about three years, and then only for Southern California club races. In those days, however, club racers included some of the world's best drivers such as Richie Ginther, Ken Miles, Jack McAfee, Bill Krause, and Ed Kretz. The track was built in the Malibu Hills near Agoura, California, on what was Paramount Studios' back lot. The "gold" grass and oak trees make the track recognizable because it has been the site of many motion pictures from the 1940s and 1950s.

The real track was just over two miles around with 11 numbered corners, although turns 6 and 7 seem to be one turn. There was an article on the track in the December 1956 issue of *Sports Car Graphic* magazine that appeared just after the track was built. The plan of the track in the article shows a somewhat different configuration that was actually the proposed track. The diagram is patterned after the track as it was built. All of the corners were banked a few degrees because the track was built as a race track, and not a converted road.

Paramount Ranch Track 9 x 12 for Scalextric and SCX

To model car racers of the 1960s and 1970s, Paramount is a place they know about because it was the subject of a series of articles in *Car Model* magazine that described, step-by-step, how to route the slots and build the track from chipboard. I built the track, took photographs, and wrote the articles for the magazine, and held the weekly races on the track. The track also appeared in the 1967 Van Nostrand

The 9 x 12-foot two-lane Scalextric version of the Indy F1 Grand Prix Track. The track is designed to allow the addition of two more lanes, to produce a four-lane track, by adding two lanes outside the curve to the right and inside all the curves to the left of the overpass.

book *Model Car Racing*, and has become a kind of icon. I have seen photographs of a half-dozen recreations of Paramount from around the world, but Rich Kozinski's track is probably the best known. This version for Scalextric, SCX, or Ninco track has much of the shape of the real track, and fits in a 9 x 12-foot space. I opted to run the straight track under the overpass to avoid a hump on the fastest part of the track. Some of the turns from the real track are missing to allow the track to fit in the available space.

Paramount Ranch Track 9 x 12 for Carrera

With this version, I wanted to fit the longest-possible straight-away into the available space which resulted in turns 2 and 3 being on the "wrong" side of the track. It made sense to simply reorient the turn numbers to the "backwards" configuration. Similar to the Scalextric/SCX/Ninco version, there was no room for turns 4 and 5, and turns 6 and 7 are combined. This is really a mirror-image version of the Paramount Track, which was needed to fit in the space. Also, the main straight is the underpass, rather than the overpass of the real track. This was changed to make sure the 1/32-scale cars without magnets would not become airborne down the highest-speed portion of the straight-away. The good news

is that the track is virtually identical to drive on as the Scalextric version or the hand-routed version I made decades ago. The real Paramount Ranch Track only had a 35-foot difference between the lowest and highest points on the course. It did not have a turn like the "Corkscrew" from Laguna Seca that dropped 190 feet. The way the 1/32-scale Carrera version had worked out, the curves that make up the Corkscrew already existed. I tried the track with just flat curves and determined the Corkscrew was

the best way to lose the elevation gained by using half of the Carrera Crossover bridge.

Indy 500 Speedway

The Indianapolis Motor Speedway may be the most famous race track in the world thanks to the Indy 500 race for IRL open-wheel cars and the Brickyard 400 for NASCAR sedans. The track is 2.6 miles around and each of the four corners is banked so speeds on the straight-aways exceed 200 miles per hour for both IRL and NASCAR cars, and even the NASCAR can turn 175-plus mile-per-hour laps.

Indy 500 Speedway Four-Lane 5 x 9 for Scalextric and SCX

The 1/32-scale track, like the real Indy 500 circuit, is basically a rectangle. It is designed to fill a 5 x 9-foot *continued on page 81*

The 9 x 12-foot Indy F1 Grand Prix Track assembled with Carrera track, and with the Carrera borders painted green and beige. This track is also designed to allow two more lanes to produce a four-lane track by adding two lanes outside the curve to the right and inside all the curves to the left of the crossing bridge.

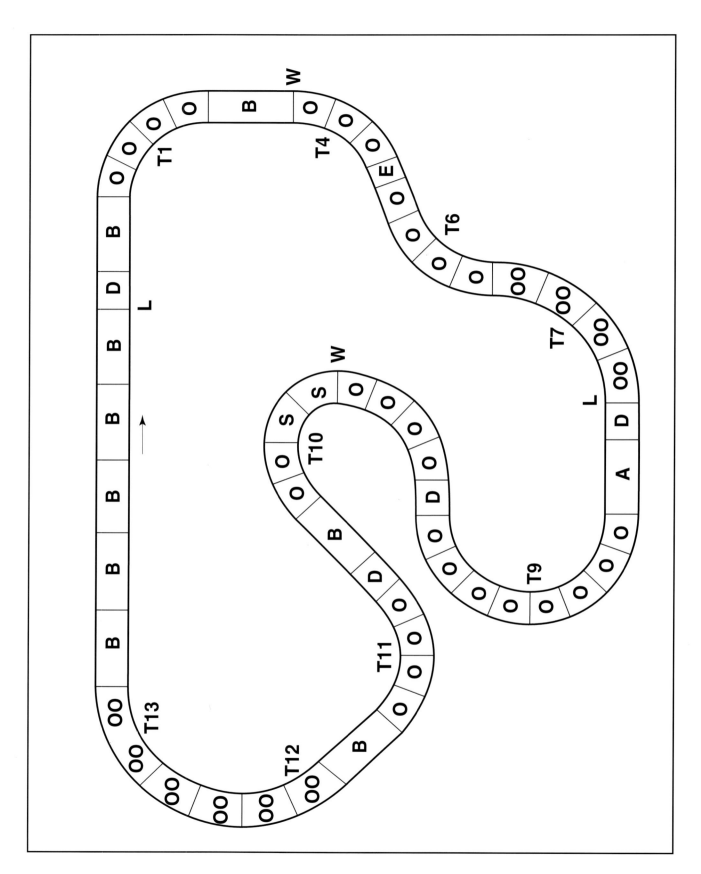

List of Scalextric or SCX Track Required for 9 x 12-Foot Indy F1 Grand Prix Track

(A list of the part numbers for the track sections and their borders that are identified by the "Key" letters on this plan is shown in Chapter 7.)

Key	Quantity	Description
H	0	1/2 Standard Curve
S	2	Standard Curve
O	28	Outer Curve
OO	10	Outer-outer Curve
E	1	1/4 Straight
D	3	1/2 Straight
B	9	Full Straight
V	0	Crossover Track
A	1	Connector Track
C	0	Chicane (lane-narrowing) Track
L		Track can be expanded in length by adding matched pairs of straight track sections here.
T		Turn numbers (correspond to real race course).
W		Track can be expanded in width by adding matched pairs of straight track sections here.
X		Track can be expanded diagonally here by adding matched pairs of equal-length straight track sections.
Y		Track can be expanded diagonally here by adding matched pairs of equal-length straight track sections.

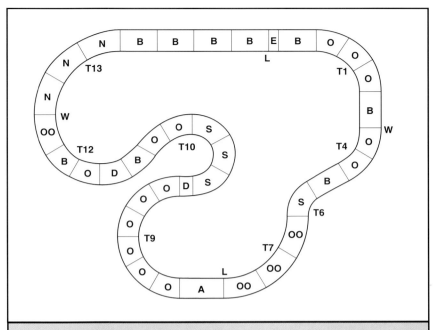

List of Carrera Track Required for 9 x 12-Foot Indy F1 Grand Prix Track

(A list of the part numbers for the track sections and their borders that are dentified by the "Key" letters on this plan is shown in chapter 7.)

Key	Quantity	Description
H	1	1/2 Inner Curves
S	4	Inner Curve
K	0	Banked Inner Curve
O	17	Middle Curves
M	0	Banked Middle Curve
OO	4	Outer Curves
N	3	Banked Outer Curve
E	1	1/4 Straight
D	1	1/3 Straight
B	6	Full Straight
Q	0	Overpass Bridge
R	0	1/2 of Overpass Bridge
A	1	Connector Track
C	0	Chicane
L		Track can be expanded in length by adding matched pairs of straight track sections here.
T		Turn numbers (correspond to real race course).
W		Track can be expanded in width by adding matched pairs of straight track sections here.
X		Track can be expanded diagonally here by adding matched pairs of equal-length straight track sections.
Y		Track can be expanded diagonally here by adding matched pairs of equal-length straight track sections.

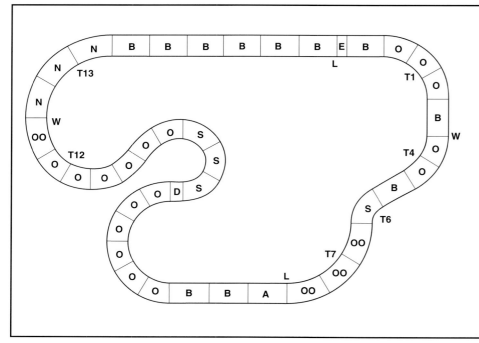

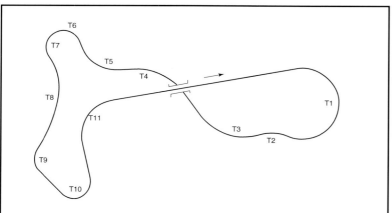

Center

The Paramount Ranch track in the Malibu Hills of Southern California is one of the few real tracks in the world that actually had a figure-8-style crossing bridge. The real track divided turns 6 and 7 into two different turns.

Bottom

The Paramount Ranch Track is assembled from Scalextric track on a 9 x 12-foot tabletop. The track can be expanded to four lanes by adding an SCX outer-outer curve to the right side and a variety of Scalextric and SCX curves and straights inside the loop to the left.

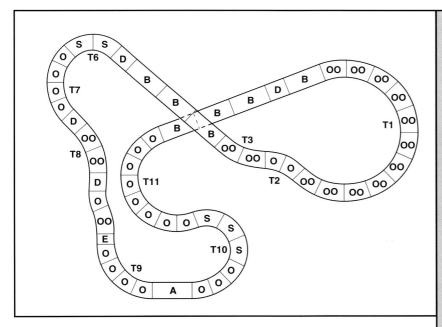

List of Scalextric or SCX Track Required for 9 x 12-Foot Paramount Ranch Track
(A list of the part numbers for the track sections and their borders that are identified by the "Key" letters on this plan are shown in chapter 7.)

Key	Quantity	Description
H	0	1/2 Standard Curve
S	5	Standard Curve
O	22	Outer Curve
OO	16	Outer-outer Curve
E	1	1/4 Straight
D	2	1/2 Straight
B	7	Full Straight
V	0	Crossover Track
A	1	Connector Track
C	0	Chicane (lane-narrowing) Track
L		Track can be expanded in length by adding matched pairs of straight track sections here.
T		Turn numbers (correspond to real race course).
W		Track can be expanded in width by adding matched pairs of straight track sections here.
X		Track can be expanded diagonally here by adding matched pairs of equal-length straight track sections.
Y		Track can be expanded diagonally here by adding matched pairs of equal-length straight track sections.

The Paramount Ranch track is assembled from Carrera track with the borders painted as described in chapter 6. Two more lanes can be added to the outside of the curve to the right and two more lanes inside the curves to the left to expand the track to four lanes.

area. Each of the corners use the SCX outer-outer curves and either Scalextric or SCX outer curves. You could prop-up the center of each of these curves to provide a simulated banking. The track can be extended, as can all the others in this book, by adding matched pairs of equal-length sets of straight tracks at WW and LL, so you could fill a garage floor with a much closer-to-scale Indy track.

Indy 500 Speedway Four-Lane 5 x 9 for Carrera

The Carrera version of the Indy 500 utilizes the standard and outer curves at each corner. There are chicanes along one straight-away so the cars can simulate the drafting moves of the real NASCAR stock cars when one car tucks behind the other to get a wind-induced "tow" so both cars achieve higher speeds. That does not work in 1/32 scale, but the sight of

one car tucking-in behind the other certainly looks like a drafting move.

Darlington Raceway

Darlington is typical of the genuine oval tracks on the NASCAR circuit in having banked turns. What is not typical is that the two turns are different sizes. Darlington's track makes an excellent prototype for a simple six-lane track that will fit on a 5 x 9-foot table using 1/32-scale track.

Darlington Raceway Six-Lane 5 x 9 for Scalextric, SCX, or Ninco

SCX offers an outer-outer curve that can be used with either SCX or Scalextric outer curves and standard curves to make a high-speed six-lane oval. If you wish, you can even elevate the corners slightly to simulate true banked turns. Ninco offers their own standard, outer, and outer-outer

Top
The ess curve at turn 6 on the Carrera Paramount Ranch track ("T6" on the plan) can be assembled with conventional curves like this to produce a flat, slightly off-camber turn.

Center
The ess curve at turn 6 on the Carrera Paramount Ranch track can also be assembled using the "Corkscrew" series of track sections described in chapter 7. The two flat standard sections in the middle of the turn are replaced with two banked standard sections to create the corkscrew effect.

Below
This four-lane Scalextric track has the rectangular shape of the Indy 500 Speedway. There are no trick track sections and no ess bends—just racing action.

Top
The ess curve at turn 6 on the Carrera Paramount Ranch track ("T6" on the plan) can be assembled with conventional curves like this to produce a flat, slightly off-camber turn.

Center
The ess curve at turn 6 on the Carrera Paramount Ranch track can also be assembled using the "Corkscrew" series of track sections described in chapter 7. The two flat standard sections in the middle of the turn are replaced with two banked standard sections to create the corkscrew effect.

Below
This four-lane Scalextric track has the rectangular shape of the Indy 500 Speedway. There are no trick track sections and no ess bends—just racing action.

curves so the track can be duplicated with Ninco track as well. A NASCAR track is an excellent place to use chicanes on the straights. Scalextric and SCX both offer straight chicane tracks that continue the single-file for as many sections of straight chicane track as you wish. By placing a set of chicanes on each pair of lanes, you get the visual effect of the cars drafting each other nose-to-tail down the straight just as they do on the real NASCAR tracks.

Darlington Raceway Six-Lane 5 x 9 for Carrera

Darlington is a great prototype for a Carrera six-lane track because you can actually have two different turns on a 1/32-scale high-speed oval. The banked turn at one end simulates the broader of Darlington's two turns, while the flat six-lane turn at the opposite end of the 1/32 scale effectively simulates Darlington's tighter curve. There's no reason why two banked turns or two flat turns couldn't be used on both ends of the track. However, the combination of one banked and one flat turn makes for very interesting racing. I've fitted chicanes to the four inner lanes, but they could be fitted to all six lanes so the cars can simulate the drafting typical of every NASCAR race.

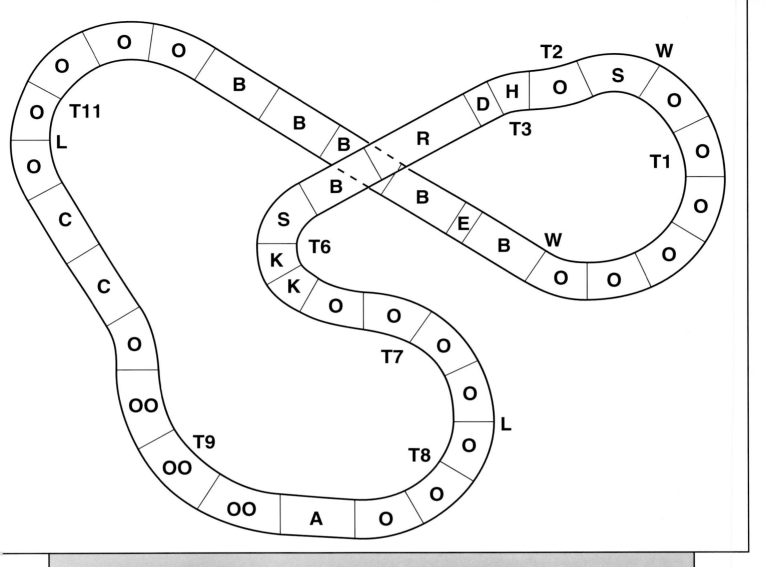

List of Carrera Track Required for 9 x 12-Foot Paramount Ranch Track

(A list of the part numbers for the track sections and their borders that are identified by the "Key" letters on this plan is shown in chapter 7.)

Key	Quantity	Description
H	1	1/2 Inner Curves
S	2	Inner Curve
K	2	Banked Inner Curve
O	20	Middle Curves
M	0	Banked Middle Curve
OO	3	Outer Curves
N	0	Banked Outer Curve
E	1	1/4 Straight
D	1	1/3 Straight
B	6	Full Straight
Q	1	Overpass Bridge
R	0	1/2 of Overpass Bridge
A	1	Connector Track
C	2	Chicane
L		Track can be expanded in length by adding matched pairs of straight track sections here.
T		Turn numbers (correspond to real race course).
W		Track can be expanded in width by adding matched pairs of straight track sections here.
X		Track can be expanded diagonally here by adding matched pairs of equal-length straight track sections.
Y		Track can be expanded diagonally here by adding matched pairs of equal-length straight track sections.

The four-lane Carrera version of the Indy 500 Speedway also fits on a 5 x 9-foot ping-pong table. This one has a pair of chicanes down the back straight so the cars can simulate the "drafting" moves that are common to NASCAR and IRL open-wheeled racing.

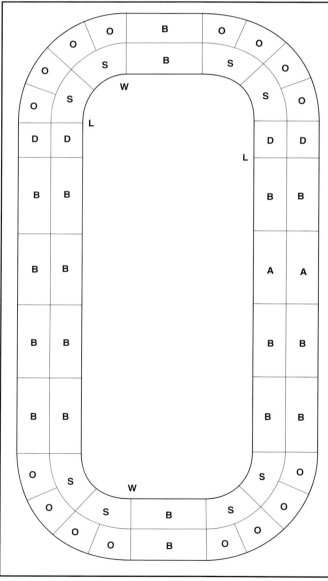

List of Scalextric or SCX Track Required for 5 x 9-foot Indy 500 Speedway

(A list of the part numbers for the track sections and their borders that are identified by the "Key" letters on this plan is shown in chapter 7.)

Key	Quantity	Description
H	0	1/2 Standard Curve
S	8	Standard Curve
O	16	Outer Curve
OO	0	Outer-outer Curve
E	0	1/4 Straight
D	4	1/2 Straight
B	18	Full Straight
V	0	Crossover Track
A	2	Connector Track
C	0	Chicane (lane-narrowing) Track
L		Track can be expanded in length by adding matched pairs of straight track sections here.
T		Turn numbers (correspond to real race course).
W		Track can be expanded in width by adding matched pairs of straight track sections here.
X		Track can be expanded diagonally here by adding matched pairs of equal-length straight track sections.
Y		Track can be expanded diagonally here by adding matched pairs of equal-length straight track sections.

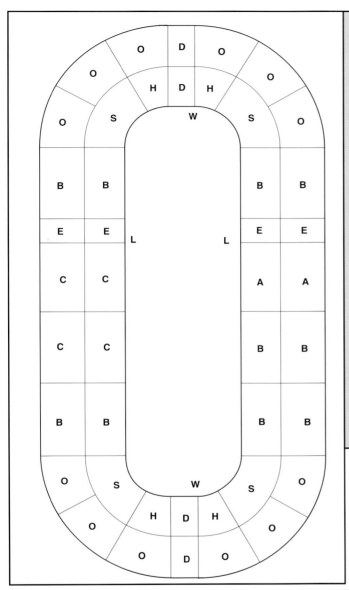

List of Carrera Track Required for 5 x 9-Foot, Four-Lane Indy 500 Speedway

(A list of the part numbers for the track sections and their borders that are identified by the "Key" letters on this plan is shown in Chapter 7.)

Key	Quantity	Description
H	4	1/2 Inner Curves
S	4	Inner Curve
K	0	Banked Inner Curve
O	12	Middle Curves
M	0	Banked Middle Curve
OO	0	Outer Curves
N	0	Banked Outer Curve
E	4	1/4 Straight
D	4	1/3 Straight
B	10	Full Straight
Q	0	Overpass Bridge
R	0	1/2 of Overpass Bridge
A	1	Connector Track
C	0	Chicane
L		Track can be expanded in length by adding matched pairs of straight track sections here.
T		Turn numbers (correspond to real race course).
W		Track can be expanded in width by adding matched pairs of straight track sections here.
X		Track can be expanded diagonally here by adding matched pairs of equal-length straight track sections.
Y		Track can be expanded diagonally here by adding matched pairs of equal-length straight track sections.

Six lanes of 1/32-scale racing can be fit into just 5 x 9 feet of space. This is the Scalextric and SCX version of the Darlington Raceway. Only SCX makes the outer-outer curves, but either Scalextric or SCX can be used for the rest of the track. The track can be assembled with Ninco track, but it will require another foot of length and width.

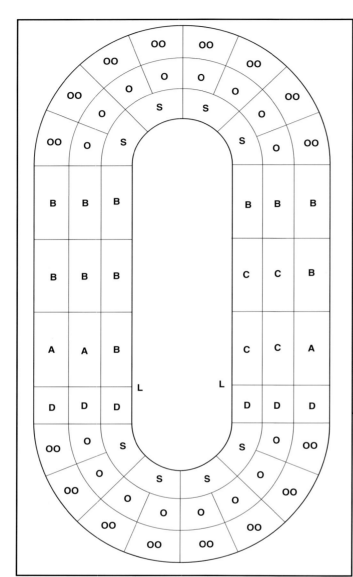

List of Scalextric or SCX Track Required for Six-Lane 5 x 9-Foot Darlington Raceway

(A list of the part numbers for the track sections and their borders that are identified by the "Key" letters on this plan are shown in Chapter 7.)

Key	Quantity	Description
H	0	1/2 Standard Curve
S	8	Standard Curve
O	16	Outer Curve
OO	16	Outer-outer Curve
E	0	1/4 Straight
D	6	1/2 Straight
B	11	Full Straight
V	0	Crossover Track
A	3	Connector Track
C	4	Chicane (lane-narrowing) Track
L		Track can be expanded in length by adding matched pairs of straight track sections here.
T		Turn numbers (correspond to real race course).
W		Track can be expanded in width by adding matched pairs of straight track sections here.
X		Track can be expanded diagonally here by adding matched pairs of equal-length straight track sections.
Y		Track can be expanded diagonally here by adding matched pairs of equal-length straight track sections.

The Carrera banked turns can be used for one end of an oval like this 5 x 9-foot Darlington Raceway, or both ends. The banked turn on one end means the cars will run faster through that turn than through the flat turn which is what happens at the real Darlington Raceway because the two banked turns have different diameters.

When two cars enter the chicanes, one must tuck in behind the other. It's the same effect you see when real race cars tuck in behind one another to execute what's called a "drafting" maneuver where both cars have more speed because of the improved airflow over the two cars.

Six cars thundering through a banked turn is an exciting sight, even in 1/32 scale. Carrera offers the three different sizes of curves necessary for banked turns. The curves are useful on road racing courses because they allow different-speed corners to be built into the course.

List of Carrera Track Required for 5 x 9-Foot Six-Lane Darlington Raceway

(A list of the part numbers for the track sections and their borders that are identified by the "Key" letters on this plan is shown in chapter 7.)

Key	Quantity	Description
H	0	1/2 Inner Curves
S	3	Inner Curve
K	6	Banked Inner Curve
O	6	Middle Curves
M	6	Banked Middle Curve
OO	6	Outer Curves
N	6	Banked Outer Curve
E	6	1/4 Straight
D	0	1/3 Straight
B	11	Full Straight
Q	0	Overpass Bridge
R	0	1/2 of Overpass Bridge
A	3	Connector Track
C	4	Chicane
L		Track can be expanded in length by adding matched pairs of straight track sections here.
T		Turn numbers (correspond to real race course).
W		Track can be expanded in width by adding matched pairs of straight track sections here.
X		Track can be expanded diagonally here by adding matched pairs of equal-length straight track sections.
Y		Track can be expanded diagonally here by adding matched pairs of equal-length straight track sections.

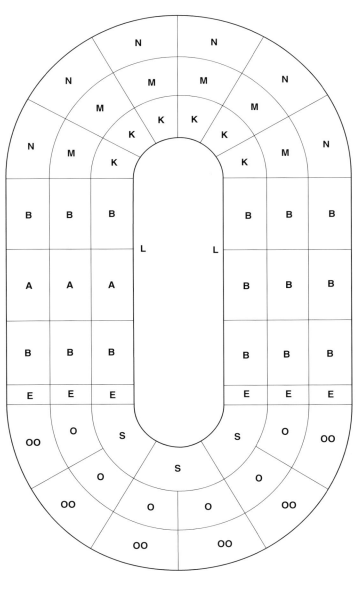

9 HO RACE CARS

The Johnny Lightning "Thunderjet 500" series of friction-powered cars have lightweight plastic bodies, attached with screws so they will fit onto a T-Jet or Model Motoring Thunder Plus chassis. This is the Thunderjet 500 1970 Barracuda, the Buick Grand National, and the 1940 Willys.

The sight of a matchbox-size model zinging around the track like a mad humming-bird is, to many racers, the very best of model car racing. These HO-size racing cars are small enough so they can be raced in a relatively small space with the track dwarfing the cars, rather than the cars dominating the track as they tend to do with 1/32-scale cars. These HO-scale cars are usually faster than the larger 1/32-scale cars. Most modern HO cars have very strong magnets that allow the cars to corner faster than most 1/32-scale cars too. The HO cars are so fast that they almost seem to be achieving the speed of a full-size

racing car—reduced to scale, their speeds exceed 300 miles per hour. The good news is that, thanks to those strong magnets and well-designed controllers, you can actually control these almost bullet-fast projectiles.

HO Scale?

All of the cars that race on the 3-inch-wide tracks are referred to as HO racing cars. The letters "HO" are used by model railroaders to define models built to 1/87 scale. The original HO motorized automobiles of the 1960s were 1/87- or HO-scale models of full-size Fords and Chevrolets so the vehicles could become animated portions of a model railroad layout. That

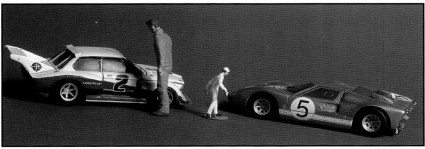

Both of these cars, an Aurora/Tomy A/FX BMW 3.0 CSL and a Boye Racing Models Ford GT40 MkII body on a Mattel 440-X2 chassis, are HO scale. The cars are close to 1/58 scale. The figure next to the BMW is the closest accurate-scale person you can buy to match these cars. The figure is a Preiser 1/50-scale construction worker, and the figure next to the Ford GT40 MkIII is a Preiser 1/87-scale (true HO-scale) mechanic.

HO-scale (1/87-scale) mechanics that look fine with the HO sedans, including the Fairlanes and Impalas. Mattel's diecast Hot Wheels Racing series and the Winner's Circle diecast scenes include some 1/64-scale pit crews and officials that look right with the Tauruses, Luminas, Grand Prixes, and Intrepids. Preiser offers 1/50-scale mechanics in orange overalls that are superb figures and fit well with the 1/58 sports and GT cars.

Collectible HO Race Cars

A large collector market for HO-scale cars exists out there. It is perhaps even more active than the

concept lasted until someone realized the cars could be raced. When the hobby of model car racing developed, the manufacturers, notably Aurora and Tyco in America and Faller in Europe, made replicas of actual racing cars such as Ferraris and Corvettes. They had determined that the chassis under the 1/87-scale Ford and Chevrolet sedans was the smallest that could be made and still sell the cars for a price customers would be willing to pay. As a result, the manufacturers made new bodies to fit the standard chassis. Frankly, there is no common scale for any of the mass-produced HO cars. The "Pony Cars," including Mustangs, Camaros, and Barracudas, are about 1/64 scale, while sports and GT cars such as the Corvettes, Cobras, Jaguars, and Ferraris, are about 1/58 scale. Ironically, the real Formula One and Indy cars have become so large in the past decade or so that the HO versions are about 1/72 scale, which is close to the original HO scale.

Today, model car racers realize that a true 1/87-scale Corvette, Cobra, or Ferrari electric racing car would be too small to have visible detail, and certainly too small for easy parts replacement. For most HO racing enthusiasts, the size and detail are not a problem. The size is not bothersome except when additional scenery is needed. For example, how large should the pit crew figures be? Preiser produces true

The new Model Motoring cars are re-creations of the traditional Aurora HO cars of the 1960s and include a new "Thunder Plus" chassis. Here are Model Motoring's 1969 Camaro, 1967 Pontiac GTO, 1969 Pontiac GTO, and 1966 Mustang. The models are offered in a wide choice of colors.

The Mini-Models series of handcrafted Nu-Rora cars includes this 1969 Camaro and 1963 Falcon Futura. The Futura is available as either a coupe or convertible in a variety of super detail and paint combinations.

Pictured are some of the more popular HO racing chassis from Joe Furuli's collection. The chassis in the front row are the most common examples including (left to right): Life-Like "M" Fast Tracker, Mattel (ex-Tyco) 440-X3 "pan" for NASCAR cars, Mattel (ex-Tyco) #440-X3 Formula One, and Tomy A/FX Super G-Plus. Life-Like has replaced the "M" chassis in all their cars with a new "T" chassis that has a smaller, but much more powerful motor. The racing chassis shown in the second row are no longer in production although the Aurora Thunderjet (or T-Jet) is still available as new original stock from R. E. H., and a similar Thunder-Plus chassis is being manufactured by Model Motoring. The older chassis include (left to right): Aurora Slimline, Aurora Thunderjet, Aurora early A/FX, and Aurora A/FX Magna-Traction.

market for 1/32- or 1/24-scale cars. Far more HO-scale sets than 1/32-scale sets were sold in the 1970s and 1980s, so more children raced this type of car. Today, those kids are adults and they want their toys back. You do not need to bother searching eBay or flea markets for HO cars, because nearly all are being produced today as reproductions of the originals, or as brand-new cars styled to match original Aurora or Tyco models. This is especially good news for those who would rather drive their model racing cars rather than stack them in boxes.

Nearly all of the HO cars are produced in relatively limited numbers so they are still very collectible. The standard advice applies: If you want to collect, buy a second car and keep it as an "investment" so you can race the first car without the guilt that can come from the thought of destroying your investment.

Model Motoring HO Race Cars

Aurora's Thunderjet really kicked off the HO-scale racing market in 1963. Prior to that, most HO cars were adaptations of designs intended to be motorized road cars that were accessories to model trains. Aurora originally called their cars "Model Motoring" to clarify what this new toy was designed to be. Model Motoring exists today as a separate company (with no connections to Aurora) that produces re-creations of the original Aurora cars right down to a re-creation of the pancake-style Thunderjet or T-Jet chassis (called a "Thunder Plus"), and re-creations of the Aurora "Snap-Lock" track that uses dime-size

U-shaped clips to hold the track sections together. Even today, very few modelers use the new Model Motoring cars with their model trains. These cars are raced just as in the 1960s.

Aurora HO Race Cars

The NOS (New Original Stock) Aurora Thunderjet chassis from R.E.H. and Model Motoring's Thunder-Plus have a similar chassis style. A variety of bodies are available for these chassis, including many cast-resin replicas of original Aurora bodies, new injection-molded plastic bodies, and friction car bodies designed to screw onto the Thunderjet (T-Jet) or Thunder-Plus chassis. The "Thunderjet 500" cars from the Johnny Lightning division of Playing Mantis are toy cars with injection-molded

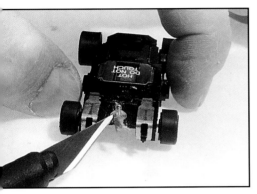

Left top
Life-Like is using this "T" chassis under all of their newer cars. It is designed to be at least a match for the Mattel 440-X2.

Left bottom
To tune-up an HO chassis, remove any lint from around the guide pin and be sure the pin is not worn or bent.

Right top
Use a pipe cleaner or a toothpick wrapped with a thin rag or paper towel to remove any excess grease or oil from around the gears, motor, and wheel bearings.

Right
Snap out the pickup shoes and inspect the springs to be sure they are the same length. Polish the areas where the pickup shoes pivot on the chassis to insure good electrical conductivity.

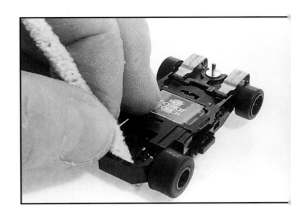

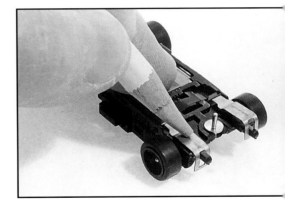

Use a hard rubber typewriter eraser to clean and polish the rubbing surfaces of the pickup shoes.

plastic bodies and friction chassis. The bodies are attached to the toy chassis with screws and will fit right onto the T-Jet chassis from Aurora or Model Motoring. For a more realistic vehicle, it may be necessary to trim a portion of the chassis to lower the body to a more realistic position. The Mini Models Nu-Rora series offers fully-painted and detailed HO classics including a 1963 Ford Falcon Futura hardtop or convertible, and a 1969 Z-28 Camaro.

Aurora also offered the pancake-style chassis as a "Magna-Traction" car with an extra magnet plate to provide magnetic attraction to the pickup rails on the track. The magnetic system became a standard for HO scale, but the later G-Plus and A/FX cars with separate inline-style motors far outperformed the old Magna-Traction cars. Stronger magnets and gold- or silver-plated pickup shoes and motor brush holders are available from BSRT, Slotech, Wizard, and others for the T-Jet chassis.

Tomy A/FX HO Race Cars
Tomy produces A/FX and other cars from original and upgraded Aurora molds and offers three distinct inline-motor chassis beneath a variety of bodies. The Super G-Plus chassis included in most of their race sets have two long, black magnets between the inside of the rear tires and the corners of the motor's magnets. The Tomy A/FX Turbo chassis have black square-shaped magnets located between the wheels and the metal plate that surrounds the motor. The fastest motor and strongest magnets are in the Tomy A/FX SRT chassis that utilizes two small but shiny rectangular magnets between the inside of the rear tires and the corners of the sheet metal motor case. The A/FX Turbo and A/FX SRT cars have a separate motor, and the motor in the Tomy G-Plus cars is an integral part of the chassis. BSRT offers replacement motors for the Super G-Plus and G-Plus.

Tyco HO Race Cars
Mattel offers the 440-X2 chassis under the Formula One cars and most of the NASCAR cars. Mattel purchased the Tyco product line in the early 1990s, and many of the less-expensive "Formula Tyco" cars with weaker magnets and slower motors are still available.

Tyco introduced the faster 440X-2 chassis in the 1990s, and it is still produced by Mattel, with some upgraded magnets and armatures, as the 440X-2.

Mattel HO Race Cars

The chassis used under the Mattel Formula One and Indy cars is more narrow than the one used for the NASCAR cars. The 440-X2 chassis for the NASCAR cars and some sedans has wider tabs on the sides and is often referred to as the "pan" chassis. The chassis can be adapted to fit the Formula One bodies to provide a slightly longer and more realistic wheelbase. The "Formula" and the "pan" chassis should have identical performance.

Life-Like HO Race Cars

Life-Like has produced three different HO chassis: the current "T" chassis with a separate motor and two variations of the original "M" chassis with its plated-steel motor plate cover. The older "M" chassis under the Power Tracker cars has stronger magnets and a faster motor than the older "M" chassis under the "Fast Tracker" cars, but the two chassis appear to be identical. However, take a closer look and you'll see that the armature segments (the steel plates that hold the copper wire windings on the armature) in the Power Tracker motor are angled or "skewed" in the Fast Tracker, while the armature in the Power Tracker is straight like the armatures in all other current production cars from Tomy and Mattel. The "T" is much faster, has stronger magnets, and is more reliable than any of the earlier Life-Like cars. The "T" also offers a performance that's a match for the Mattel 440-X2 cars.

Tune-Ups

The term "tune-up," to any racer, simply means checking all the components of the car to be sure each is perfect. Start with the wheels and tires to see that no lint or hair is wound around the axles (or the guide pin) to cause friction. Clean out any dirt or lint with a pipe

The race car transporters and pit scenes from the diecast series of scenes from Racing Champions and Hot Wheels can be used to provide incredibly realistic scenery for any HO NASCAR track. This is Shawn Lee's "Shawnadega" tri-oval.

Mattel's Formula One Ferrari, McLaren, and Jordan flash by a pit scene from a Hasbro 1/64 scale Winner's Circle collectible diecast toy pit scene from their NASCAR series.

cleaner. Apply a single drop of plastic-compatible oil to each bearing and wipe away any excess oil with a clean pipe cleaner or a piece of facial tissue wrapped around a toothpick. Clean any excess grease from the gear teeth, apply new plastic-compatible grease, and wipe away any excess.

Snap out the pickup shoes and be sure both coil springs are the same length. Use a typewriter eraser to scrub away any oxidation from the points where the pickup shoes pivot, and from the areas where they touch the metal pickup rails on the track. Check the shiny copper commutator on

Furuli Models is one of several firms that offer cast-resin bodies to fit T-Jet chassis including this 1966 Stepside, 1966 Panel Delivery, and 1955 Pickup.

the armature (the rotating portion of the motor) to be sure it's clean. You can clean it with a toothpick dipped in lighter fluid or lacquer thinner. Keep the solvent or lacquer thinner away from the copper wires on the armature. Clean the commutator outdoors and dry it thoroughly before operating the car. Finally, check the guide pin to be sure it is not worn flat or bent.

Spin the front wheels to make sure the tires and wheels are round, and if necessary, gently bend the wheels until they are running true. Place the car on the track and lift the rear so enough throttle can be applied to gently spin the rear wheels to check them for true-running. The rear tires can be sanded round by holding a piece of fine-grit sandpaper face up on the track while gently lowering a running car onto the sandpaper. Finally, check to make sure the body fits properly so there's no chance the tires will rub against it.

Troubleshooting

The first task in problem solving is to see if the problem lies in the car, track, or controller. If just one car is having trouble, the problem is most likely on that car. Next, perform all of the tune-up steps outlined above to be sure that the entire chassis is ready to function properly. Usually if an

HO car does not run, the problem can be traced to the pickup shoes. Be certain both pickup shoes are touching the track, and that both pickup shoe springs are in place. Next, look at the commutator (the shiny copper portion of the rotating part of the motor). The two motor brushes that contact the commutator must be in place, and if they are not, install new motor brushes. Trace the metal path the electrical current must follow from the pickup shoes to the motor brushes to be certain that there are no bent tabs or broken metal parts that would interrupt the flow of current to the motor brushes. If the motor can be removed, try a motor from another car to determine if the problem lies with the motor or the chassis.

Racing Secrets

I'd love to be able to tell you that it's the clever car builder/tuner who wins the races, but it's seldom true with this hobby. Most of the "secrets" are no longer secrets, and this hobby is about realistic racing, and not just racing. Here are some helpful racing secrets:

- Be sure the tires are completely round and touching the track.
- If the rules allow, sand the tires so the magnets clear the rails by the thickness of a business card.
- Be sure the pickup shoes are free to move without binding.
- Be sure the pickup shoes are level across the width of the track and that they are touching the pickup rails on the track.
- Be sure there is no more than a paper-thickness of sideways movement of either the front or rear axles.
- Use a hobby knife to carefully shave the body-mounting clips inside the body so the chassis can rattle beneath the body (this helps isolate any vibrations so they are not amplified to induce tire-hop).
- Be sure the armature is shiny and free from oil.
- Be sure the pickup shoes are shiny.
- Check the guide pin to be certain it is not worn flat or bent.
- Oil the bearings, grease the gears, and wipe away any excess oil or grease.

This 1932 Ford pickup, five-window coupe, and 1933 Ford three-window and open-motor hot rod bodies are cast-resin to fit on the T-Jet chassis from Furuli Models.

The BSRT series of sports and GT cars have nearly as much detail as the similar 1/32-scale cars. The models have modified T-Jet chassis without magnets so they are a delight to drift around corners.

Magnets on any car, including those on this Tomy A/FX G-Plus chassis, can be removed by gently prying between the magnet and the chassis with a screwdriver. Stronger magnets are available, but for more of a racing challenge, leave the magnets out.

HO Performance Parity

Model car racing is a hobby more than a sport. For most involved, how the car looks is at least as important as how fast it goes. For the most racing fun and action, try to race cars with equal performance. If one brand of car proves slower on your track than another, there are two choices: limit the races to just that one brand, or allow enough "hop-up" parts to be fitted to the "slower" brand so it performs equally with the "faster" brand. The second alternative can be especially helpful because it can allow a broader variety of different car bodies and paint schemes because several brands of cars can be raced in the same events.

Generally, the Super G-Plus cars are the quickest. The performance can be matched with a Mattel 440X-2 car when the 440X-2 is allowed the special silicone-coated sponge tires and wheel assemblies, threaded motor brush holders with heat sinks, and medium-strength magnets available from Wizard, Scale Auto, or Slot Tech. These

three modifications should make the Mattel 440X-2 cars competitive with the G-Plus cars. The only modification allowed on the G-Plus cars is to sand the tires to effectively lower the cars. The silicone-covered foam tires from Wizard, Scale Auto, or Slot Tech are available in a variety of diameters so you can pick a tire to lower the car as much as you dare. Similar modifications can be made to the Life-Like cars with the "T" chassis.

An alternative method to making all cars equal is to select just one brand of chassis. It's not difficult to adapt the Life-Like bodies to the Super G-Plus chassis, or vice versa. Similarly, bodies can be swapped between Mattel and Life-Like cars, especially the NASCAR cars, when thin strips of styrene are added inside the bodies and a bit of plastic is shaved from the body mounts to adapt one brand of body to another brand of chassis.

Hop-Up Power

The BSRT "Super G2" chassis is an example of how far a "stock" chassis can be modified to improve its performance. The "Super G2" is a Tomy G-Plus chassis assembled from all new components: BSRT offers the chassis fully assembled or the components can be purchased separately to assemble them yourself so you can pick and choose which components you feel are most important. The chassis itself is

modified to accept body posts to mount a clear plastic body (or the standard injection-molded plastic body can be retained) and is available with the optional stainless steel rear axle retainer. The guide pin is a Pro Guide with a stainless steel pin and an aluminum collar. The pickup shoes are a new "Ski-Shoe" shape with gold plating for maximum electrical contact. The pickup holders are also gold plated, as is the endbell that holds the motor brushes. The armature is a new "Hot Stock" component and there's a new crown gear with a choice of 20 or 22 teeth, a new pinion gear, and a special Delrin gear spacer. New double-flanged wheels are fitted with "HOTT" Silicone tires at the rear and O-ring tires on new wheels and a new axle at the front. The super-wide silicone rear tires and the ultra-thin O-ring tires detract from the realism, but they allow for quicker cornering. You can opt to use the stock wheels with BSRT standard-width Twinn-K silicone rear tires if you prefer to be realistic. All these parts are available separately from BSRT, as well as from Slot Tech, Wizard, and other manufacturers. Similar motor, chassis, and gear components are also available for the Mattel 440 X-2 cars. It's easy to spot new components (many are gold plated), so they are not the kind of thing you can try to sneak through to make your cars faster than the others.

These "hop-up" components, from BSRT as well as similar components from Pro Tech, Wizard, Scale Auto, and Slot Tech, are examples of modifications that can be made to all of the cars so they all are competitive for equal racing.

The next steps in the quest for speed are to replace the motor magnets, fit a faster armature, install stronger traction magnets and silicone-coated foam tires on aluminum wheels with a clear plastic body, and purchase a new controller with a much lower ohm rating (perhaps 5 to 10 ohms). Cars this quick are not much fun on a sectional track—they're intended for the 20-foot-long, eight-lane tracks routed from solid sheets of plastic.

NASCAR Racing

One of the most popular forms of HO-scale races are those that duplicate the American NASCAR sedans racing on oval, tri-oval, and road racing tracks from the NASCAR series. Currently, Life-Like offers a Ford Taurus, Pontiac Grand Prix, and Dodge Intrepid; and Mattel offers a Chevrolet Lumina, Ford Taurus, and Dodge Intrepid. Life-Like also offers a NASCAR Craftsman Truck Series-style pickup truck. Both companies offer the models in a variety of accurate sponsor and driver paint schemes.

Most of the current NASCAR paint schemes are available, but your favorite driver's car may not be available in your favorite brand of HO-scale car. However, it is possible to adapt different brands of bodies to different chassis so your favorite NASCAR body is on your favorite brand of HO chassis. Decals are available from most HO-scale suppliers, but none are exact matches for current NASCAR cars because all of the NASCAR racers are licensed and the license agreement is too expensive for the decal makers. Some of the classic NASCAR bodies, such as the 1970s Ford Fairlane, Dodge Daytona "wing" cars, a Chevy-like "70s Stock Car," and a Buick Grand National are available from Thunderjets or Model Motoring to fit T-Jet or new Model Motoring Thunder-Plus chassis.

Sports and GT Racing

Tomy, Life-Like, and Mattel offer ready-to-run sports and GT cars including Porsches, Corvettes, Cobras, Vipers, Lamborghinis, and Jaguars. Playing Mantis has a variety of Thunder-Jet 500 friction cars with injection-molded plastic bodies that will screw onto Aurora T-Jets or the new Model Motoring chassis. The Johnny Lightning Thunderjet 500 cars include Cobra 298 roadsters, Chevrolet Grand

Sports, Corvettes, and Vipers. There are also Camaros, Mustangs, Barracudas, Chargers, and AMC Pacers as Thunderjet 500 cars, and Life-Like has a 1970 Mustang to allow you to duplicate the "Pony Cars" or the TransAm racers of the late 1960s and early 1970s.

Dozens of clear plastic bodies exist that are modified re-creations of both current and vintage sports and GT cars that you can paint, decal, and mount on almost any HO chassis. However, it is very difficult to paint and detail a clear plastic body to match the quality of the factory-painted and pad-printed injection-molded plastic bodies.

Formula One and Indy Racing

Mattel produces a single body and matching chassis that is a replica of a late-1990s Formula One car. Mattel offers the car in a variety of accurate paint schemes, including Ferrari, Jordan, McLaren, Williams, and Jaguar. Tomy offers a 1980s-era Formula One body that has been available in a variety of paint schemes including Formula One, CART, and IRL.

Hot Rods and Musclecars

For many HO enthusiasts, it's the musclecars of the 1960s and 1970s that make the hobby appealing. Fortunately, nearly all of the original Aurora and Tyco bodies of the 1960s and 1970s are currently available from Model Motoring, Mini-Models, the Playing Mantis' Thunderjet 500 series, or as cast-resin bodies from suppliers including Furuli. Modern pickup trucks and high performance sedans are also available as well as hot rods such as Ford "Deuce" coupes, 1941 Willys (complete with flames from new Model Motoring and Thunderjet 500), and 1949 Mercury customs and three-window Ford coupes from Furuli.

Powersliding Turns

There is another way to have even more fun racing HO-scale cars. It's certainly exciting to watch HO cars shoot around the track while using magnets to defy the laws of gravity as the cars rocket

Three of Boye Racing Models' resin bodies including No. 2, a 1968 Ford GT40 MkII; No. 5, a 1964 Shelby Daytona Coupe; and No. 98, a Shelby 1965 427 Cobra roadster; powerslide around a replica of the harbor turn at Monaco on Jason Boye's Le Monzaco circuit.

A field of four Life-Like and Mattel NASCAR cars zoom by the pit stop area on one of the race tracks from chapter 10.

around the curves nearly flat-out. A real racing car would powerslide around many of those turns, and if a real racing car would exceed the traction of the tires, it would spin-out rather than flick itself across the room like a tossed coin. That dynamic realism can be achieved by racing 1/32-scale cars, and HO enthusiasts can have a similar experience by removing the traction magnets from their cars. Once the magnets are removed, the cars run very much like the older Aurora "pancake" chassis such as the Thunderjet and the new Model Motoring Thunder Plus. So, there's a "new" kind of HO racing that centers around chassis without traction magnets and more modern inline chassis with the magnets removed. The lap times are just a fraction of the times of cars with magnets, but it takes more skill to drive a car without magnets. That's especially good news for modelers who love the T-Jets. Now they can have exciting races with T-Jet or the Thunder Plus chassis fitted with Johnny Lightning, new Model Motoring, or any of the resin bodies designed to fit these pancake-style chassis.

BSRT HO Race Cars

BSRT is offering a series of HO sports and GT cars with a new chassis and motor that are designed to be as fast and quick cornering as a Tomy A/FX Turbo or Mattel 440-X2, but without the traction magnets. The BSRT car is as quick as a completely modified Aurora Thunderjet or new Model Motoring chassis, but the BSRT car is ready-to-race. The BSRT cars are designed to be raced without traction magnets. The cars are fitted with super-detailed clear plastic bodies that are painted on the outside and are as nearly well-detailed as the best 1/32-scale cars. BSRT has selected cars that are replicas of the popular sports and GT racing cars of the late 1960s and early 1970s, including a series of 1970s sports cars with a Ferrari 512S, McLaren M8B, Lola T260, Porsche 917-10, and Shadow. BSRT also offers a 1970 Trans Am Camaro and Mustang, and a series of sports and GT cars that includes a Ferrari 512M, Porsche 917, and Lola T70 coupe.

Boye's Sports and GT Bodies

Boye's Racing Models is offering cast-resin bodies that are exact 1/58-scale reproductions of some of the most popular sports and GT cars of the 1960s and 1970s. The Boye bodies are designed to snap onto a Mattel 440-X2 chassis. They can be modified to fit a G-Plus or Life-Like chassis but it's really not worth the trouble. The 1/58 scale was dictated by the size of the HO chassis. The wheelbase and width are very close to 1/58-scale of the real cars that are the prototypes for the Boye bodies. Bodies currently available include 1966, 1967, and 1968 Ford GT40 Mark IIs; 1964 and 1965 Cobra Daytona coupes; 1964 289 Cobra and 1965 427 Cobra roadsters; a 1967 Lola T70 Mark III coupe; and 1961 250LM, 1967 330P4, and 1967 412P Ferraris. The bodies are unpainted and the windshields are molded into the body. The simplest way to paint the body is with Floquil's model railroad "Grimy Black" color, and then mask the windshield and paint the remainder of the body. When the decals are placed on the body, apply a coat of Testors Model Master Clear Gloss to protect the decals and provide a glossy surface for the windows.

10

HO RACE TRACKS

Some model car racers focus completely on the cars once they've built a track to suit their needs or to fit in their available space. For other racers, it's almost as much fun to create, build, and learn about new race tracks as it is to drive the cars. Either way, you'll want to design or select a track design as a place to start racing. I strongly suggest you try at least three different track designs before deciding which one to keep. Even then, you always have the option of changing the track if you become bored, or your interests in cars change from road racing courses for sports and GT cars to tri-ovals for NASCAR sedans.

Quick Track-Building

You can assemble any HO track in this book in less than a half-hour and take it apart in even less time. The track is strong enough so it will hold together on the floor, but it's more fun, especially with HO cars, to elevate the

Four of the Hasbro Winner's Circle-brand diecast racing pits are lined up for this pit scene. The diecast cars have been removed and HO-scale racing cars from Life-Like and Mattel have been put in their places. Hot Wheels Racing offers similar scenes. The figures are 1/64 scale.

Uphill, downhill, and through the esses racing on the door-size "Neubauer" HO track.

The different brands of HO track are not interchangeable. This is the Life-Like track (left) and Tomy A/FX track. Different brands can be used to assemble the track by using 3-inch-long adapter track sections.

track so the cars can be seen without the need to lay on the floor. If the track needs to be kept on the floor, you will discover that the track will eventually separate at the joints from accidental slaps as you frantically grab for a deslotted car to continue the race. If you want a stronger system for holding the track sections together on the floor, stick a 4-inch piece of duct tape across the bottom of the track at each joint. The track itself provides the mechanical electrical connection, and the duct tape just keeps the track from disengaging.

Selecting the Best Track

All of the popular brands of HO track easily clip together so it takes little effort to assemble a track. Carefully consider what track to select when you buy additional pieces. First, decide if you really want a four-lane track, if two would be enough, or if you want a minimum of six lanes. Take a look at the tracks in this chapter and in chapter 11 and notice that some tracks have banked turns and others have large 15-inch-radius turns or tight 6-inch-radius turns. The chart of available track on page 100 shows that only Tomy A/FX and Life-Like offer four-lane banked turns (a 9-inch-radius bank and a 12-inch-radius bank) and that Tomy A/FX and Model Motoring exclusively offer the larger 15-inch-radius turns and the smaller 6-inch-radius turns. A track made from nothing but flat 9- and 12-inch turns is nowhere near as exciting to drive on as one that incorporates banked turns and/or those hairpin 6-inch turns and broad 15-inch turns.

The Life-Like track probably has the best locking system that is easy to assemble and disassemble, but holds together securely. Unfortunately, Life-Like only offers a limited selection of track sizes. Mattel's track is a compromise, but is available in even fewer sizes. However, most of the original Tyco track as NOS (New Original Stock) can be found through a dealer. The dealer can order the track through R.E.H. Dis-

tributors. The Model Motoring track is great for avid early-Aurora fans who want the track to match the cars. The Model Motoring track works best when mounted permanently to the tabletop. The Tomy A/FX track is probably the easiest to assemble and disassemble, but the disadvantage is that the track can accidentally work itself apart. The most fanatical HO racers seem to select Tomy, but they go two major steps further and mount the track permanently to a tabletop and solder each and every joint between the pickup rails together, or they remove the rails completely and install continuous new rails for each lane.

Mixing Brands

None of the four popular brands are interchangeable, but Life-Like offers 3-inch-long adapter track sections that can be used to combine Life-Like, Tomy A/FX, and Mattel track. So far, there are no adapters for the Model Motoring track to join with Tomy, Mattel, or Life-Like track. The 3-inch adapters for Life-Like can usually be fitted into a track so you could use all Life-Like or all Mattel (or Tyco) track for the 9- and 12-inch-radius turns and most of the straights with adapters, where needed to transition to Tomy A/FX four-lane (9- and 12-inch radius) banked turns or to the 6-inch or 15-inch turns. Tomy A/FX offers the largest selection of curves and straights, and their track sections were used for all tracks that appear in this book.

Racing on the High Banks

All of the HO cars that have traction magnets can negotiate a flat turn as quickly as a banked turn. The banked turns help the end of the track resemble a real raceway, particularly if the track is one of the super speedways such as Daytona or Darlington. Only Tomy A/FX and Life-Like offer a 9-inch and a 12-inch banked turn so their track has to be used for any four-lane banked turns. It is necessary to have at least 15 inches of straight track, but 30 inches is better, to twist the track from the banked turn back to the flat. If the track is an oval with banked turns at each end, the straight-aways should be at least 45 inches long.

Assembling a Raceway

The geometry of the track is extremely simple so the track will fit together nicely and align properly. The standard curve sizes are 6-, 9-, 12-, and 15-inch radius, and the standard sizes for straight tracks are 3, 6, 9, 12, and 15 inches long. What's amazing, especially to 1/32-scale enthusiasts, is that all the popular brands of HO-scale track are 3 inches wide. Every track arrangement is workable in 3-inch increments.

You can enlarge or expand almost any track plan by inserting pairs of equal-length straight track sections on opposite sides of the track. Those locations are marked with the letters "W" and "L" on the plans featured in this book. If you study other published plans, you'll see how they can be enlarged. It's also possible to decrease the size of some tracks by removing equal lengths of straight track from opposite sides of the track. The three track plans in this chapter are designed for a 2 x 6-1/2-foot space, but by removing 18 inches of track from the long parallel straightaways, the tracks can be squeezed into a 2 x 4-foot area.

How Much Track Do I Need?

Look at the quantity of track sections required for each track to see precisely how many track sections and what sizes are needed to build each of these plans. Note the largest quantity required for each track section in this chapter and in chapter 11 and collect at least that many pieces of that size so there's enough track to build any race track in this book. You'll be able to build an almost infinite assortment of plans from other sets and have enough track sections to design your own race tracks.

Most HO race car sets include a number of track plans you can assemble with the track in the set. The

Tomy "Super International Race Set" even includes plans so you can duplicate 18 of the world's Formula One tracks using just the track pieces in the set. Sets are relatively inexpensive sources of lots of track. It's far less expensive to buy a large four-lane set than to buy individual track pieces. Often there will be cars in the set for "free" because the savings are so great. Having said that, even the Tomy International set only includes a single piece of 15-inch-radius track and no banked turns at all. I recommend you buy two sets of Tomy's 9-inch and 12-inch banked turns, and two circles of their 15-inch curves to supplement the track in the largest of four-lane sets. Look for examples of just how to use those banked turns and 15-inch curves in chapter 11.

Maintaining a Race Track

All the brands of HO race track sections are rugged and much stronger than typical 1/32-scale track sections. The track requires very little maintenance. Dust the track with a clean, lint-free cloth before each race. Use some of the track cleaning fluid sold for model railroads to clean the pickup rails about once a month. When the track surface stays

The original Aurora track with U-shaped clips to hold the track together is now being produced by Model Motoring.

dirty even after you dust it, use plain soap and water to clean the track. Never clean the track with any solvent that could melt or damage the plastic. Polish the rails with a hard rubber eraser like those sold for cleaning model railroad track. Vacuum the slots once in a while, especially if the track is being operated on the floor.

Troubleshooting Track

Problems with model race car tracks can usually be traced to just

This figure-8 track is assembled as a portable layout with felt covering a 2-1/2 x 6-1/2 foot door. The door is supported on a pair of sawhorses. The pits are from Hasbro's Winner's Circle and the trees are Life-Like model railroad accessories.

Track Section Key to the HO Track Plans

Each of the plans in this book has letters on the track sections so you can identify which track sections are required. This chart will help you see which pieces are used and the part number of each piece available. Remember that you can mix brands as long as you can buy an adapter track that will join the two brands you are using, but that you must include that 3-inch adapter track in your plans.

Key to the HO Scale Track Sections

Key	Description	Tomy	Life-Like	Mattel (Tyco)	Model Motoring
E	3-inch Straight	8632	none	"K"	none
D	6-inch Straight	8641	none	5830	none
C	9-inch Straight	8622	9930	5629	9452
B	15-inch Straight	8621	9934	5836	9405
A	15-inch Terminal	8627	in set*	5832	9453*
J	6-inch Curve	8656	none	none	9451
H	9-inch Curve** 90°	8623	9927	5831	none
I	Half 9-inch Curve**	8624	none	5846	9408
K	9-inch Bank Curve	8628	9929	5852	none
G	12-inch Curve	8642	none	5844	9407
M	12-inch Bank Curve	8991	9928	none	none
F	15-inch Curve	8663	none	none	9406

On the race track plans, the letters L, W, X, and Y are places where matched pairs of straight track can be inserted to expand the size of the track for a larger space.

*NOTE: The Tomy A/FX terminal track is 15 inches long, but the Life-Like, Mattel (Tyco), and Model Motoring terminal tracks are 9 inches long, so an additional 6-inch straight track must be used to join with the 9-inch terminal track to make a 15-inch-long pair of track sections. The 6-inch straight will have to be added to the quantity of track needed for those three brands.

**NOTE: All of these plans are drawn using half-9-inch curves (45-degrees of a circle) to make it easier to see the different sizes of curved track required. You can substitute 90-degree 9-inch curves for most pairs of these 45-degree curves.

Adapters
(all are 3-inch straights)

	Tomy	Life-Like	Mattel (Tyco)	Model Motoring
Tomy (A/FX) to Life-Like	none	9931	none	none
Mattel (Tyco) to Life-Like	none	9932	none	none
Tomy (A/FX) to the older Aurora Snap-Lock track	8626	none	none	none

---

one car. However, if you find that more than one car has a problem, it could be the fault of the track, controller, or connection to the track. Swap controllers to see if that solves the problem.

If the problem is a stalled car, it could be the fault of the track, particularly if several of the cars stall at the same place. If you have a problem with just one section of the track being "dead," remove it and check the joints between its pickup rails and the rails of adjoining tracks to be sure they are bent so they do not maintain contact.

The only other problem you may encounter with HO track is a broken aligning tab that can occur if you tried to force the track apart when disassembling it, or if the track was stepped on. Broken HO tracks can usually be cemented back together with five-minute epoxy. The epoxy joint should be as strong as the track.

Race Track Design

All HO sectional track has steel rails so the traction magnets in the cars will hold the cars to the track. Most HO race tracks are designed to use the magnetic grip to their maximum advantage. The corners are laid out so a relatively steady throttle position (perhaps full-on, perhaps only partially "full-on") can be held. With large curves and relatively short straights, it's possible to design a race track that can be driven

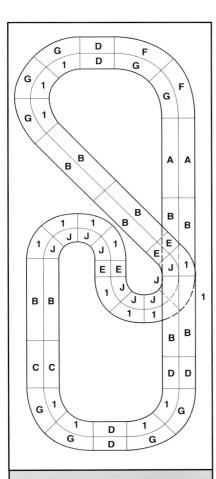

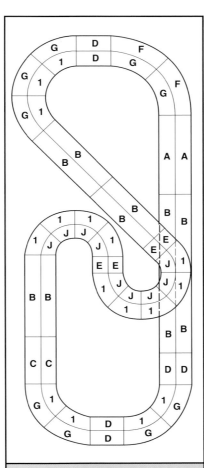

This figure 8-style-style is designed to fit in a 2-1/2 x 6-1/2-foot area. If different track sections are substituted on the two parallel straights, 18 inches can be removed and the track can be squeezed into a 2 x 4-foot space. It's an adaptation of the 5 x 9-foot "Neubauer" 1/32-scale track.

Track Sections Required

Key	Quantity	Description
E	4	3-inch Straight
D	6	6-inch Straight
C	2	9-inch Straight
B	10	15-inch Straight
A	2	15-inch Terminal
J	9	6-inch Curve
H	0**	9-inch Curve 90º
I	16	Half 9-inch Curve
K	0	9-inch Bank Curve
G	9	12-inch Curve
M	0	12-inchBank Curve
F	2	15-inch Curve

Disconnect the track sections at the overpass from the previous track to remove the "figure-8" pattern. Also move the overpass or bridge supports. This is an interesting track to race on thanks to the tighter ess-bend and a much longer straight than the previous plan.

Track Sections Required

Key	Quantity	Description
E	4	3-inch Straight
D	6	6-inch Straight
C	2	9-inch Straight
B	10	15-inch Straight
A	2	15-inch Terminal
J	9	6-inch Curve
H	0**	9-inch Curve 90º
I	16	Half 9-inch Curve
K	0	9-inch Bank Curve
G	9	12-inch Curve
M	0	12-inch Bank Curve
F	2	15-inch Curve

around with nothing but full throttle. Conversely, it is possible to have straights that are too long, and too many curves so the driver has to constantly pump the throttle like a late-1800s telegraph key. The best race track design lies somewhere between those two extremes.

If you have an HO-scale electric race car set, you already have some idea of what's fun and not fun about driving around the track. Ask 15 HO-scale model car racers what they consider the "best" track design, and you will likely get 15 different opinions. Some people prefer high-speed courses that are the HO-scale equivalent of Daytona's tri-oval or the Indy 500 rectangle. The cars can be driven at virtually full-throttle except for a very calculated and precise lift-off of the throttle just as you enter the curve. The challenge here is to maintain as much of that straight–away speed for as far as possible into the corner without flipping the car. This is very much the challenge that drivers of the real cars face. Other HO-scale racers prefer race courses that meander about so much they can almost get lost on the track. The task is to discover each corner and deal with it as a somewhat unpredictable challenge.

The figure-8 is a popular shape for model car race tracks because it provides equal lane lengths. If you've actually raced on a four-lane figure-8, only the two outer and two inner lanes are equal. If a few curves are added to either end of the figure-8, the equality disappears. The best way to provide equal racing is to divide the race into four equal "heats" as described in chapter 13, so that every driver has equal time on every lane. The figure-8 still offers an interesting track design because it provides an excuse for the cars to climb and descend a hill, and it's fascinating to watch the cars pass over and under each other.

Advanced Race Track Design

I encourage hobbyists to assemble their own track designs. Frankly, it's far easier to "design" an HO track with the track sections themselves

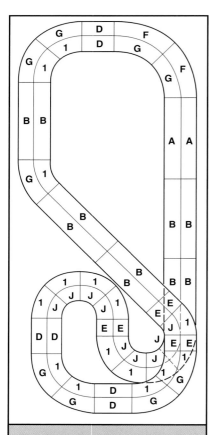

This plan includes the best features of the two previous tracks in this chapter. The track and bridge supports have been repositioned so the overpass is at the end of the straight. There is still the tight ess bend and the table-length straight like the previous track, but the figure-8 pattern makes racing on each lane more equal, and the corkscrew-like downhill spiral looks exciting.

Track Sections Required

Key	Quantity	Description
E	6	3-inch Straight
D	4	6-inch Straight
C	0	9-inch Straight
B	10	15-inch Straight
A	2	15-inch Terminal
J	9	6-inch Curve
H	0**	9-inch Curve 90 degree
I	16	Half 9-inch Curve
K	0	9-inch Bank Curve
G	9	12-inch Curve
M	0	12-inch Bank Curve
F	2	15-inch Curve

than it is to work it out on paper or with a computer. The project can start with the designs in the set or those in this book, but try other combinations. Computer design packages are available on the internet if more help is needed. The simple 3-inch-width and 3-inch variations in curve radius and straight track length make it easy to align track sections even if the track wanders all around a door-size table. When you come to the place where the tracks are supposed to make the final connection to complete the track circuit, don't be discouraged if the tracks do not align. Usually, the sections will be out of line by some combination of 3-inch increments. If not, be sure every joint is fitted snugly together and tracks that are supposed to run parallel to the sides of the table really do so. You can have some odd misalignment if you run tracks diagonally, but here you can bring that misalignment into something correctable with a 3-inch larger or smaller curve radius, or 3 inches more or less straight by adding or subtracting track sections from the diagonal path.

The Neubauer Raceway

These three race tracks are examples of how you can develop a track design. This layout is an adaptation of the "Neubauer" plan for 1/32-scale cars from chapter 7. I developed the first version by moving track sections around on the table-top. It has the figure-8-style configuration of the 1/32-scale Neubauer race track. The problem is that the longest straight-aways are only 30 inches in length. The track wasn't fun to race on because there was no place to let the cars wind-out to top speed. I liked the looks of the up and over ess-bends, so I simply re-arranged the straight tracks to create a 51-inch straight-away without the figure-8 shape. This track is really the most fun on which to race. Still, it was annoying to have my vision interrupted as the cars flashed down the middle of the straight. I thought there must be a way to get a long straight and still have a figure-8, so I

modified the circuit into its final form with the figure-8 at one end. This straightaway was only 6 inches shorter than the previous circuit's, and the track over the end of the straight-away was not as annoying because it did not hide the cars for as long. You can see more of the hidden track if you drive from the straight-away side of the track.

It is also possible to modify any of these plans to avoid using track sections such as the 6- or 15-inch-radius curves that are only available from Tomy A/FX. For example, a 15-inch curve can be replaced with a 12-inch curve and a 3-inch straight attached to each end of the curve to make up the difference. If you substitute 9-inch curves for 6-inch curves, the layout will be 3 inches longer and wider for each 9-inch curve used to replace a 6-inch curve. You can make up the difference where a 9-inch curve has replaced a 6-inch curve by inserting 3-inch straight tracks on the sides.

Design Your Own Race Track

New racing circuits can be designed by simply being willing to change whatever bothers you about the track you've assembled from a plan in the set or from one of the plans in this book. If you like any of the plans in this book, they can be enlarged to fill greater spaces if equal lengths of straight track are added at the letters "L" and "L" along the length of the track, or "W" and "W" along the width of the track. Parallel tracks, like those marked "LL" and "WW", can usually be found on any track plan to enlarge them to fit a greater space.

Race Track Design Priorities

When you have raced on a variety of tracks, you'll probably find certain elements of each track you prefer, and others you can live without. This is my personal list of priorities (in order of importance to me) for race track design for HO race tracks:
• All parts of the track within 36 inches of the edge to reach deslotted cars easily.

This track was assembled with Tomy A/FX track using the track section sizes in the chart. Extra straight track sections are used to display cars that are not currently being raced.

- Guardrails around the edges of the skid aprons/borders to keep cars off the floor.
- Separate power packs for each lane.
- The longest straight possible in the space.
- Large-diameter curved track sections wherever possible.
- Skid aprons/borders for the outside of every piece of curved track to provide the option of racing cars without magnets.
- Banked curve to "extend" the length of at least one straight.
- An uphill and downhill section somewhere on the track.

Borders for Powersliding Cars

If you enjoy powersliding cars without magnets around the corners, there's bad news: Borders for any brand of HO track simply don't exist. If the track is mounted to a tabletop with screws, borders can be made with two layers of HO-scale model railroad cork roadbed, but the borders must be nailed or glued to the tabletop. An alternate method of making borders is to cut them from two layers of hard-surfaced countertop material such as Masonite. However, there is no way to clip these borders to portable track sections, so they must

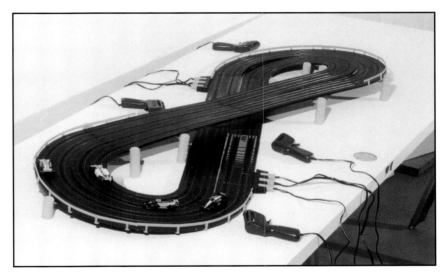

A standard-size 2-1/2 x 6-1/2-foot door, supported by folding sawhorses, makes an excellent permanent but portable table for HO-scale race tracks. This is a basic four—lane figure-8 with 9- and 12-inch radius curves.

also be nailed or screwed to the tabletop. Alternatives are to build a four-lane track and the cars without magnets will only powerslide on the center two lanes, or build a six-lane track and race cars without magnets on the center four lanes. These options leave the outer lanes to be used as skid aprons. If you like this system, you

can paint the lanes green to simulate grass, or beige to simulate a sand trap as shown in chapter 6. If you opt for this system of using track for the borders, you may want to cut some borders to match the length of the 15-inch curves so the largest curves available in HO scale can be utilized. The two layers of Masonite or

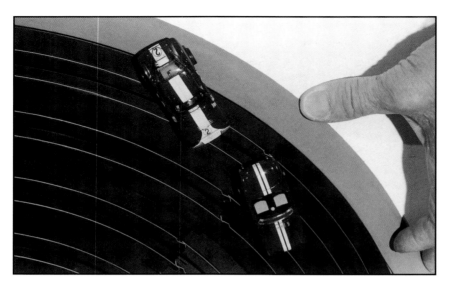

hardboard can be permanently cemented together to the outside ends of the 15-inch-radius turns because there is nothing else to run around the outside of the large-radius curves.

Tables for HO Tracks

The easiest table for HO race tracks is an interior door. Doors are available in 24-, 30-, and 36-inch widths, and most are 6-1/2-feet tall. Purchase the lightest-weight 2-1/2- or 3-foot door you can find, as well as a pair of folding sawhorses. Some sawhorses are made of stamped-metal channels so 2 x 4s can be inserted into the legs to raise the height of the table if you want to have more than the 30 inches of height from standard sawhorses. Smear a thick layer of silicone bathtub caulk on the bottom of the table (door) where the sawhorses will

When you powerslide HO cars without traction magnets, the cars need room to drift out from the turns without hitting a guardrail or falling off the track. On the outer lanes, skid aprons or borders are needed. This border is two layers of HO-scale model railroad cork roadbed. The roadbed can be fastened to the tabletop with silicone caulking compound.

This 4 x 12-foot four-lane track was assembled using 6-, 9-, and 12-inch radius curves. The ess bends have skid aprons and borders made from HO-scale cork roadbed. The turns at the ends of the straights are walled with sheet styrene glued to the edges of the track.

If you are racing mostly sports and GT cars, they are about 1/58 scale. Preiser offers sets of painted figures in 1/50 scale that are the right size for HO sports and GT car scenes. The top row includes figures in the Preiser number 68212 Mechanics set, and the bottom row is the Preiser No. 68203 Passers-By set.

touch the table. Also smear a thick layer of caulk on the top of the sawhorses. The caulk will provide a simple nonslip surface so the table won't fly off the sawhorses. If the caulk is not enough, the stamped metal sawhorses can be attached to the table (door) with bolts, nuts, and large fender washers.

The Permanent Raceway

I don't recommend you attach the track to the tabletop. Part of the fun of racing model cars is being able to change the track when you've learned to drive the existing track with consistently quick lap times. The easiest way to hold the track to the tabletop is to drape a large sheet of felt cloth over the tabletop as shown in the photographs of the finished tracks in this chapter. The felt will grip the track enough to keep the track from sliding across the tabletop. Buy green felt if you want to re-create a real race track in America's southern states or the hills of England or Germany; or buy beige if you want to re-create a track in Spain, California, Arizona, or Nevada. Cloth stores sell felt in 2-yard widths. An approximate 3-1/2 yards of felt is a large enough piece to cover a ping-pong table.

Another method is to use a latex-base caulking cement, such as Liquid Nail's Projects and Foamboard cement or Chem Rex PL300 Foam Board Adhesive, to hold the track to the tabletop. Lay the track where you want it and run a bead of the cement along the outer and inner edges of the track. Hold the track in place with books or other weights while the cement dries overnight. When you decide to change the track, slice through the bead of caulking with a steel spatula and pry the track loose.

Race Track Realism

If you're willing to mount the track permanently to a tabletop, use the same scenery techniques for model railroads—plaster-soaked paper towel scenery shapes included. However, do not use any kind of loose material to add texture to the scenery because it can be picked up by the cars that slip off the track into the scenery. If you want a textured surface, buy paint fillers that create non-skid surfaces. These fillers can be mixed into standard latex paint so the scenery can be painted green for grass, beige for dirt, or a combination of the two.

Plain green or beige felt makes excellent scenery that won't damage the cars. Hills can be made from wadded-up newspaper stuffed beneath the felt. The felt is also portable so you can change the track without changing the scenery. Use trees with flexible plastic trunks and large clumps of lichen moss for the leaves. Avoid using trees that have loose ground foam or sawdust particles to simulate leaves.

The Mattel Hot Wheels Racing, Racing Champions, and Winner's Circle diecast cars are offered with pit scenes that include a pit wall, tools, jacks, and other details as well as uniformed pit crew. The people are about 1/64 scale, which is about right for the HO NASCAR cars. If you want a crew or corner workers close to the size of the 1/58-scale cars, use the 1/50-scale construction workers and spectators available from Preiser. The 1/64-scale trucks and race car transporter trailers are also available from various makers of diecast cars with the racing logos of the major NASCAR teams and some are available for Indy and Formula One teams. Model Motoring produces Aurora injection-molded plastic kits for a two-stall pit stop, curved bleachers, and a grandstand with a press box on the roof.

11

REAL HO RACE TRACKS

Four HO-scale replicas of NASCAR cars flash by the pits on the four-lane version of the Indy 500 Speedway track. The cars include Life-Like's model of Jeff Burton's No. 99 Exide Ford Taurus, Life-Like's model of Mark Martin's number 6 Valvoline Ford Taurus, Life-Like's model of Chad Little's No. 97 John Deere Ford Taurus, and Mattel's model of John Andretti's number 43 Cheerios/STP Pontiac Grand Prix car. The cars in the pits are all included in the series of Hasbro Winner's Circle diecast metal model dioramas. The diecast models can be replaced with HO racers as shown in chapter 10.

Model car racing is an incredibly realistic hobby. The HO cars are reasonable re-creations of the real racing cars, especially the paint and lettering schemes. The cars "drive" very much like real race cars with similar flip-and-roll crash consequences if the throttle is used too much. One particular advantage of HO model car racing is that the track is small enough that a replica of real track can fit into a reasonable space.

Real Raceways in HO

The HO-scale cars accelerate so quickly that they reach top speed in just a few feet. If you want to re-create the plan of a real race course with HO track, this is very good news because you'll have plenty of room for a long enough straight-away in a reasonable amount of space. Tomy illustrates 18 replicas of the world's Formula One race courses in their International set, and the largest track can be built in a 4 x 7-1/2-foot space.

Expanding Existing Track Plans

Any published plan can be expanded infinitely. Locate two parallel straight-aways on the plan and insert as many lengths of straight track as you can to expand the track. The areas where additional

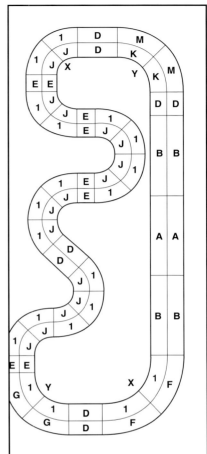

An HO-scale adaptation of the Indy Formula One Grand Prix track using Tomy A/FX track sections on a standard 2-1/2 x 6-1/2-foot door. Note that turn 13 (upper right) is banked as it is on the real track.

The plan for the HO Indy Formula One Grand Prix Track to fit a 2-1/2 x 6-1/2-foot area.

Track Sections Required

Key	Quantity	Description
E	8	3-inch Straight
D	8	6-inch Straight
C	0	9-inch Straight
B	4	15-inch Straight
A	2	15-inch Terminal
J	16	6-inch Curve
H	0**	9-inch Curve 90º
I	18	Half 9-inch Curve
K	2	9-inch Bank Curve
G	4	12-inch Curve
M	2	12-inch Bank Curve
F	2	15-inch Curve

straight track sections are inserted are marked "W" and "L" on the track plans in this book.

One advantage to the simple 45- and 90-degree geometry of HO track is that the geometry makes it easy to enlarge or reduce the size of the track without having places where the track does not align. The disadvantage of the system is that it makes it difficult to match the exact shape of most real tracks because real tracks are not confined to 45-degree turns. Areas to expand the Indy F1 and the Paramount Ranch layouts diagonally are marked with the letters "XX" and "YY".

Indy F1 U.S. Grand Prix Track

The real Indianapolis Formula One track is routed around the infield of the Indy 500 track for 2.6 miles through 13 turns. About half of the course consists of the front straight-away and the first turn of the Indy 500 race for IRL cars, but the Formula One race runs in the opposite direction so that turn 1 is now No. 13. The track is huge, and if it is built in 1/72 scale (the scale closest to the size of the Mattel and Tomy A/FX Formula cars), the track would be about 220 feet around

and require a 40 x 60-foot space. It would be difficult to build curves large enough, and even if the curves could be built, the cars would simply fly around the track at full speed. The "secret" in designing a model race track is to incorporate the feel of the real track so an amount of throttle proportionate to the drivers on the real track is used. Frankly, the largest curves available for HO scale are not nearly large enough to accomplish that. The next best thing is to duplicate the shape of the track as close as possible so the driver can lift-off of the throttle at the same time the drivers on the real track would apply their brakes. The cars will be accelerating through and out of the curves at about the same relative speed as the drivers on the real track.

Here is the Indy F1 track as it would appear with the largest available curves. I've fitted the 9- and 12-inch Tomy A/FX banked track sections to turn 13 to simulate the one-banked turn on the full-size track. The remainder of the track is a series of ess bends in more-or-less the same sequence as those on the real track. The turns on the real track are shown on the diagram in

The HO version of the Paramount Ranch track on a 2-1/2 x 6-1/2-foot door. Green felt drapes the table to simulate scenery and keep the track sections from sliding around. The bridge is supported for the full length of the straight so there is no chance the cars will jump out of the track at the top of the overpass. On the real track, the straight was level and the road passed beneath the straight.

The twisty end of the HO Paramount Ranch track. The trees are Life-Like "Giant Green Shade Trees" that use clumps of lichen moss to simulate leaves and flexible self-supporting plastic trunks.

Ranch was just over 2 miles long, which is about 190 feet in 1/58 scale. A dead-accurate model of this track would need about 25 x 65 feet of space. It is possible to come close to the actual shape of the Paramount Ranch track with HO track sections, and there are more of the real track's corners than was possible with the Indy F1 track. If you build this track, make the elevation of the main straight-away overpass as gentle as possible so the cars without magnets can accelerate down the straight at full throttle without becoming airborne.

Darlington Raceway

The real Darlington Speedway is one of the prime tracks on the NASCAR racing circuit. Its two turns are slightly different sizes, and that is not possible to re-create with HO track. The only four-lane banked curves available are 9- and 12-inch radius. It's also not possible to make an HO version of the Daytona or Talladega tri-ovals with HO track because of the minimum 45-degree bend in the curved track sections. The best you can hope for is to build a track that looks more like a triangle than an oval, especially with the limitations of the relatively tiny banked turns. The HO Darlington is an example of a very popular track configuration with HO racers. The straight-aways can be any length—I've seen them up to 20 feet long. With stock gears, HO cars will hit top speed in just a few feet, so there's no real need for an extra-long straight-away.

chapter 8. There was not room enough to include all the turns on the real Indy F1 Grand Prix track, but the ones on the HO version that closely match those on the real track are numbered to correspond to the appropriate turns on the real track.

Paramount Ranch Track

The real Paramount Ranch Track became a parking lot in the 1970s and is now long gone. It remains in the memories of many model car racers as strongly as the memory of a GTO. Paramount

Four NASCAR cars run on the Paramount Ranch track in the opposite direction of the sports and GT cars.

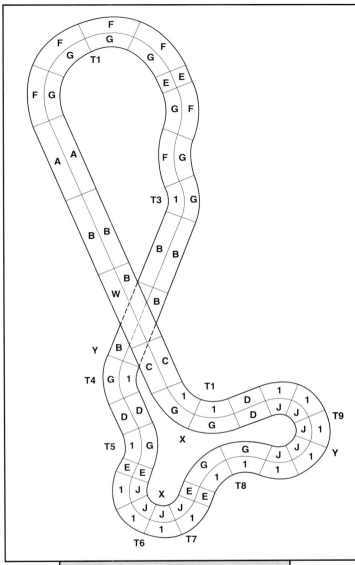

Indy 500 Speedway

Indy is one of the best-known race tracks in the world. It is 2.5 miles around— about the same length as the Formula One Grand Prix road course. An HO version would require the same 40 x 60 feet of space as the F1 track, and would be just as dull to watch. The four-lane version and first six-lane versions are a bit small, but they fit nicely on a 2-1/2-foot (wide) door. If a 3-foot (wide) door is used, the largest version can be assembled using the 15-inch curves for the outside lanes and avoiding those hairpin-tight 6-inch curves. If you're an Indy 500 fan and have the space, I'd suggest expanding the track into a 3 x 6-1/2-foot track by using 15-inch straight track sections on each end with at least four 15-inch straight track sections for each long straightaway. The largest version requires 45 x 90 inches and fits nicely on a 4 x 8-foot sheet of plywood. Another alternative is to fit 9- and 12-inch banked turns at each corner with enough room to fit two pieces of 9-inch straight track at each end of the track to allow the track to flatten out between the two banks.

The Paramount Ranch track in 2-1/2 x 6-1/2 feet for HO cars.

Track Sections Required

Key	Quantity	Description
E	6	3-inch Straight
D	4	6-inch Straight
C	2	9-inch Straight
B	8	15-inch Straight
A	2	15-inch Terminal
J	9	6-inch Curve
H	0**	9-inch Curve 90 degrees
I	16	Half 9-inch Curve
K	0	9-inch Bank Curve
G	13	12-inch Curve
M	0	12-inch Bank Curve
F	6	15-inch Curve

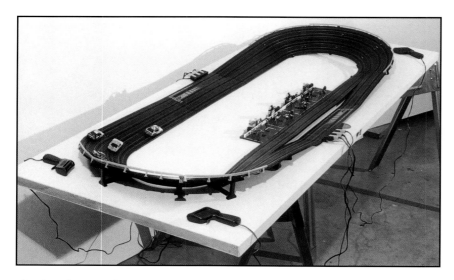

The four-lane Darlington Raceway is assembled with Tomy A/FX 9- and 12-inch-radius banked turns at each end and three 15-inch straight track sections down each straight-away to fit the track on a standard-size door. The sagging middle 15-inch straight track sections on the outer lanes can be supported with overpass supports or duct tape to the bottoms of the adjacent lanes.

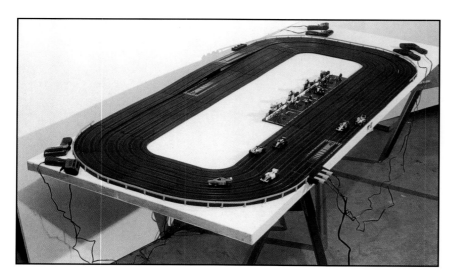

The HO version of the Indy 500 track can be assembled as either a four-lane track or this six-lane track with 6-, 9-, and 12-inch-radius curves. Only Tomy offers the 6-inch curves needed for the inner two lanes, but other brands can be used for the outer four lanes. The hump in the back straight is created by the outer track being elevated to clear the plug-in terminal strip for the middle lanes. An extension cord for the terminal can be made if wires from a spare terminal track section are soldered to a standard 15-inch straight so only the wires will be routed beneath the outer lane's track to eliminate the hump.

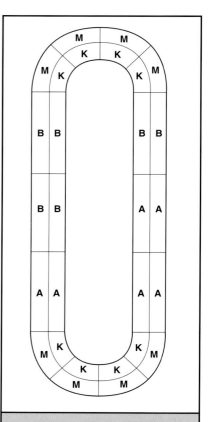

The HO-scale recreation of the Darlington high-banked oval in a 2-1/2 x 6-1/2-foot space.

Track Sections Required

Key	Quantity	Description
E	0	3-inch Straight
D	0	6-inch Straight
C	0	9-inch Straight
B	10	15-inch Straight
A	2	15-inch Terminal
J	9	6-inch Curve
H	0	9-inch Curve 90 degree
I	0	Half 9-inch Curve
K	8	9-inch Bank Curve
G	0	12-inch Curve
M	8	12-inch Bank Curve
F	0	15-inch Curve

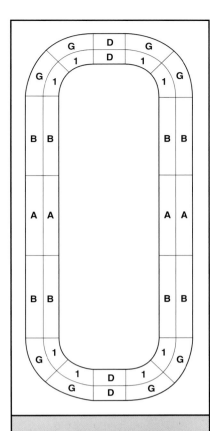

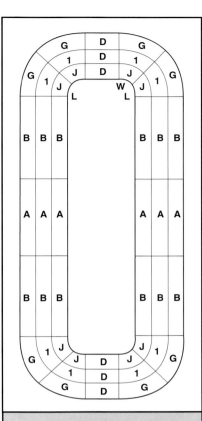

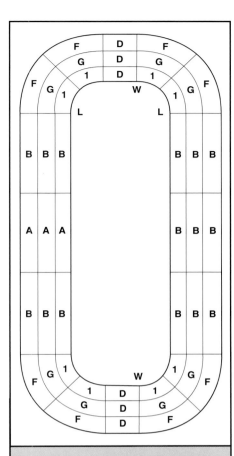

The four-lane 2-1/2 x 6-foot
Indianapolis 500 track.

Track Sections Required

Key	Quantity	Description
E	0	3-inch Straight
D	4	6-inch Straight
C	0	9-inch Straight
B	10	15-inch Straight
A	2	15-inch Terminal
J	0	6-inch Curve
H	0**	9-inch Curve 90 degrees
I	8	Half 9-inch Curve
K	0	9-inch Bank Curve
G	8	12-inch Curve
M	0	12-inch Bank Curve
F	0	15-inch Curve

The six-lane 2-1/2 x 6-foot
Indianapolis 500 track.

Track Sections Required

Key	Quantity	Description
E	0	3-inch Straight
D	6	6-inch Straight
C	0	9-inch Straight
B	15	15-inch Straight
A	3	15-inch Terminal
J	8	6-inch Curve
H	0**	9-inch Curve 90º
I	8	Half 9-inch Curve
K	0	9-inch Bank Curve
G	8	12-inch Curve
M	0	12-inch Bank Curve
F	0	15-inch Curve

The six-lane 3 x 6-1/2-foot
Indianapolis 500 track.

Track Sections Required

Key	Quantity	Description
E	0	3-inch Straight
D	6	6-inch Straight
C	0	9-inch Straight
B	15	15-inch Straight
A	3	15-inch Terminal
J	0	6-inch Curve
H	0**	9-inch Curve 90º
I	8	Half 9-inch Curve
K	0	9-inch Bank Curve
G	8	12-inch Curve
M	0	12-inch Bank Curve
F	8	15-inch Curve

12

DRIVING SCHOOL

A pair of Carrera Porsches power-slide through the ess curves on the Scalextric 5 x 9 Ascari Track.

Think of the last time you watched an automobile race, even if it was on television, and remember that strange phenomenon that often occurs; you find yourself believing you're in control of the car. You don't imagine that you are in it because you're experiencing the joy of seeing the beauty that is unique to a car in motion. You are the one doing what the driver does to brake just on the smoky side of locking the wheels; then deftly planting your foot in the throttle while you feed-in just enough steering to powerslide through the corner, you floor the right pedal, accelerate, and fishtail down the straight.

Steering with the Throttle

If you've ever raced a real car you understand that many real race cars are steered more with the accelerator pedal than the steering wheel. You use the steering wheel primarily to break the wheel's grip to set up the car for the turn. Once the steering angle is set up, the car is controlled by applying more or less pressure on the accelerator pedal and the throttle mechanism on the carburetor or fuel injection system. That driving technique was the "standard" in the 1950s and 1960s. The only difference between driving a model car and a real one is that the slot makes that initial steering

The magnets from some HO cars can be removed so they can powerslide around the corners like the Aurora Ferrari.

A Scalextric and a Carrera McLaren powerslide their way around Carrera's wonderfully broad-radius outer-outer curve. The guardrails are Carrera, but the safety barrels and signs are from SCX.

correction, and you use the hand controller to steer the car the rest of the way around the turn.

Understeer and Oversteer

When more and more throttle is applied on a real car as it is sliding around a corner, one of two things happens. The car either slides wider as the tail starts to slide out (oversteer), or the front wheels start to slide and the car tries to assume a tighter line through the corner (understeer). Modern automobiles are designed so the front tires will break away first, but older automobiles, particularly sports cars, were designed so the rear wheels slid first.

Even with a modern car, rear-wheel sliding can be induced if there is enough power in the engine to break the rear wheels loose.

Powerslides

"Powersliding" is one of the words used to describe the experience of applying so much throttle that the rear wheels break traction. It is one of the biggest thrills model car racing has to offer. A model car can powerslide around all corners. Today's model racing cars are often fitted with magnets, and the magnets can be strong enough so the front end of the car slides out (of the slot, in this case) before the rear.

The stronger the magnet, the more understeer; the weaker the magnet, the more oversteer.

Overdriving the Magnets

There hasn't been any specific reference to 1/32 scale or to HO cars because when it comes to driving, there isn't much of a difference between the big and little cars. The HO cars travel much faster, and generally are stuck much tighter to the track. The only way to control HO cars with magnets is to find the precise throttle setting that will keep the car from flicking itself across the room when the magnet's force is overcome by centrifugal force. There is also the option of racing cars without magnets such as the T-Jets or Model Motoring chassis, or the magnets can be pried out from the other brands. Without magnets, the quickest way around any corner is to powerslide at least part of the turn.

The 1/32-scale MRRC ready-to-run cars and Fly cars have magnets strong enough to hold these much heavier cars to the track almost as well as the magnets hold the HO cars to the track. The driver can overdrive the magnets to stretch the magnet's force enough to slide the cars around the larger curves such as Carrera's, Ninco's, or SCX's outer-outer curves. Virtually all other brands of 1/32-scale cars have magnets weak enough that the cars slide around or try to stay inside the point where the magnets let go and tire traction controls the car. On some tracks and in some turns, it's actually quicker to keep the car's tail tucked in so the tire traction and magnets keep it from sliding out or de-slotting. On other corners, it's quicker to apply as much power as possible so that it is just short of allowing centrifugal force to rip the guide shoe out of the slot. Experiment to determine which technique produces the fastest laps, practice until both techniques are perfected, and then race against similar cars or against the clock to see which technique produces the lowest lap times.

Some of the more popular model car controllers include (left to right): Tomy A/FX, Artin, Scalextric, Carrera, Ninco, and Parma.

The more common power packs (left to right): Artin, Scalextric, Carrera 26754 Evolution, Carrera 20731 Exclusiv, and Radio Shack 220-503.

Death-Defying Jumps

If a track incorporates an overpass or a downhill, there's an opportunity for the cars to "catch some air" as they come down the bridge. It changes the horizontal challenge of de-slotting to a vertical challenge. The best technique for keeping the car on the track must be developed with practice. If there's room before the hill, punch the throttle and then flick it off to get a combination of acceleration and instant braking to get the car moving and settle it down so it rides at least somewhere near the slot on the descent. Get it right and the feeling is very much like the "point-and-shoot" cornering

technique of throwing the car into the corner and catching it just before it can spin out of the slot, only this time the car has to be caught before it can jump too far out of the slot vertically. The 1/32-scale cars with motors in the front can be driven at slightly higher speeds down a bridge section than cars with motors in the rear. More weight could be added to the rear-motored cars, but I wouldn't recommend it. If speed is a problem, divide the racing classes into front-motored and rear-motored cars.

Point-and-Shoot Driving

Sometimes driving techniques can be matched to the track. If the track is constructed of nearly all the standard-size curves, the fastest way around may be the "point-and-shoot" driving technique. The technique for driving virtually all of the corners is the same: keep the power on until the car is as close to the corner as you dare, snap on the brakes so the tail starts to slide, and stop the slide before the car can de-slot with a gentle application of throttle. It looks like the car is rocketing from one out-of-control slide to another, and this driving method only works with cars that have medium-strength magnets or none at all.

Which Controller?

Every racing set includes a controller for each lane. Most controllers are shaped like a pistol and the speed is controlled with your trigger finger. Pistol-grip controllers are offered by Scalextric, SCX, Ninco, Artin, Tomy, Mattel, and Parma, to name a few. Some model car racers prefer the plunger-style controller, in which the controller is held like a baseball bat and the throttle controlled with your thumb. Plunger-style controls are standard from Carrera and MRRC.

The controllers are rated in ohms and are matched to the cars in the set. You may find that you have more control of cars with powerful motors such as the Fly cars if you

The Scalextric standard connector track with a three-connector 1/8-inch phone jack was installed to allow the use of controllers that apply electric braking action.

use a controller with a lower ohm rating. You may also want to try a different controller because you like the feel better. If you want a controller with a lower-than-standard ohm rating of, say, 30 or 45, Ninco's Vario and Carrera's Xtreme-Control controllers have adjustable ohm ratings so one controller can be used for any brand of car. Scalextric offers a 30-ohm controller, and Parma and MRRC offer controllers with 45, 25, and less ohms. Scalextric offers a C8052 Power & Control package for powerful cars that includes two 30-ohm controllers and their Power Base connector track with brake, reversing switch, and a second transformer.

If you want to try a controller that is a different brand from the track, you will usually have to make an adapter to connect the controller to the track. Scalextric and SCX use a standard two-conductor 1/8-inch (3.5 mm) phone jack, and Ninco has a three-conductor standard 1/8-inch (3.5 mm) phone jack, so the jacks and plugs can be purchased at an electronics hobby store including Radio Shack. A Carrera, MRRC, or Parma controller can be wired to one of the phone jacks and plugged into a modified Scalextric or SCX connector track.

Carrera and Artin have non-standard plugs and sockets that are not readily available. The plug from a Carrera or Artin controller cable can be cut and attached to a 1/8-inch (3.5 mm) three-conductor phone jack socket to the plug end and a plug to the controller end. You have just made an "adapter" cable that will allow a choice of controllers. The phone jack can be used to connect and disconnect your regular Carrera or Artin controller. You can also use that same adapter cable to plug in a Ninco or Parma controller if the jack is wired to correspond to the wire connections inside the Parma and Ninco controllers. The color coding is different on the Carrera or Artin controllers than Ninco or Parma. Since there are only three wires, the proper connections can be found by trial and error.

Plenty of Power

Each lane needs a separate electrical power supply circuit. If there is only one power supply connection, the controller on one lane can affect the controller on another lane. For example, if you are power-sliding your car around a turn at the edge of control and your competitor suddenly goes from full throttle to none to enter a corner, your lane will receive a surge of power that will send your car flying. The Scalextric, SCX, Tomy, Mattel, and Life-Like sets have a power pack that is shared by both lanes.

I strongly recommend you purchase a second connector or terminal track for your Scalextric or SCX track, and a second Scalextric or SCX power pack with about 13-volt amps per lane. I suggest the Scalextric C8066 Power Plus connector tracks. Decide which power pack is to be dedicated to which lane, and cover the controller connection with tape or a blank plug so two controllers cannot be connected to the same lane. Ninco, Carrera, and Artin have single power packs, but the circuits inside the pack are divided so each lane has its own power. You may find that the Artin power pack's 0.15 amps per lane is not enough current. The Carrera

Exclusiv power pack comes with the 1/32-scale sets and offers 14 volts with .24 amps per lane, and Ninco also offers power packs with more amps to replace the weaker Artin pack.

Experienced model car racers purchase a filtered pure 12 volts of DC power from a $40 transformer, such as Radio Shack's 220-503, for each lane. Personally, I can't tell much difference between Carrera's optional No. 20731 Exclusiv power pack with 18 volts and .6 amps per lane and the Radio Shack transformers with 13 volts and 3.0 amps per lane, but I probably could notice a difference if I were racing modified cars with faster motors and stronger magnets.

Wiring for Brakes

The Tomy A/FX, Life-Like, and Mattel HO sets do not offer brakes as standard, but the magnets in the cars grip the track with such force that they effectively act as brakes. In 1/32 scale, the Scalextric, SCX, and Artin sets don't have brakes as a standard feature. Scalextric does offer a special C8066 Power Plus connector or terminal track that has its own built-in brake feature, but the connector will only function with Scalextric or SCX controllers. Any track can be wired for brakes by using the wiring diagram in chapter 2. Brakes can be added to the controllers themselves, but it's much simpler to just buy a Ninco, Parma, Carrera, or MRRC controller that already has brakes.

To rewire the terminal track for a brake circuit, trace the wire's circuits from the controller to the track using the diagram in chapter 2. Match the wires to the connections inside a Ninco controller, and install a braking circuit in a standard Scalextric connector track. Drill a 1/4-inch hole into the side of the terminal block and fit it to a 1/8-inch (3.5 mm) phone jack socket. Look closely and you can see which part of the printed circuit board contains the terminals to connect the new wires. After the plug is installed, the Scalextric socket can no longer be used. Plug a spare phone jack into the

The additional wires needed to add brakes are red. They're installed and soldered to the Scalextric printed circuit board at the proper places to match the wiring diagram in chapter 2.

Use a separate phone jack plug or a piece of tape to blank-off the standard socket so only the new socket can be used for the lane that has the wire connections for braking.

socket so no one will accidentally try to use it. You will only need one plug per socket because you'll want a separate connector track for each lane with Scalextric and SCX so there is a separate power supply for each lane.

The wires have to be soldered in place in order to add a phone jack to any connector track. You may be able to find a hobby shop that will do the work for you, and some shops offer pre-wired track sections. With the brake circuit in place, any Ninco or Parma controllers already wired with a plug to match Ninco can be used.

13 ORGANIZED RACES

A Carrera McLaren and a Pro-Slot Ferrari in the heat of an organized race.

There are many ways to enjoy model car racing. Some racing enthusiasts like to watch the cars circulate around the track, and others prefer to see them at racing speeds but opt to keep it a personal pleasure. If you want to race two cars with just one person, the Scalextric "Pacer" system can be installed to control the second car while you race the first. Unfortunately, the system only works with Scalextric, SCX, or Ninco if the Ninco adapter track is used.

Equal Lap Length

It is not possible to make both lanes equal unless it is a simple fig-ure-8 track. The best way to make all lanes equal is to divide every race into heats, and have one heat per lane. To finish the race, drive an equal amount of time in each lane.

The length of the track can also be divided into tenths of a lap. When the race stops, the winner is the car that has completed the most number of laps and tenths of a lap. The tenths of a lap can be important because racing is often close.

Which Lane?

The most frequently asked question at any race meet is, "Which lane is mine?" The way to

The Scalextric lap counter can also be used with SCX track. It records the number of laps, buzzes at the end of the laps you determine, and provides a fastest lap time.

avoid that question is to color-code each lane, and provide matching removable stickers that can be placed on the bottom of each car. The commercial raceways provide a color stripe beside each lane for the entire length of the track. A more realistic way to color code the track is to use 1/4-inch diameter self-adhesive labels (or cut 10 1/8 x 1-inch-long strips of self-adhesive labels or colored tape) and apply them to the lanes as the indicators of tenths of a lap. The strips should run parallel to the slot, and the entire length of the inch counts as the next tenth of a lap. Use a pen to write a small number 1, 2, 3, and on to 9 and 0 on each label or strip. The zero mark will, of course, be placed at the start-finish line.

The 1/4-inch diameter dots on the 1/4 x 1-inch colored strips are visible enough so the corner marshal replacing deslotted cars can quickly find the cars. The deslotted car will have a large round color sticker on its bottom, and the corner marshals will develop the habit of picking up the car, turning it over to look at the color, and look at the track to see which color corresponds to the colored label on the bottom of the car. While the car is upside down, the corner marshal also has the opportunity to see if the guide shoe is

The Carrera lap counter uses a light beam reflected from tape. The counter includes extra tape so it can be used with any brand of track. It records fastest lap, distance, and flashes when the race is complete.

cocked to one side and needs to be straightened in order to slide the car back into the slot.

It's Time to Race

When organizing a race, a time will need to be established for the race. An accurate lap counter and a device to automatically signal the end of the race are required. Use one of the Ninco, Carrera, Scalextric, or SCX electronic lap counters that has a timer, and insist that every racer let off the throttle the minute the end of the race is signaled. Another suggestion is to buy a photography darkroom timer from a camera supply store to completely turn off the track power at whatever time you determine to be the duration of the race.

Record each driver's laps and tenths, and run the next heat and record the results. Make photocopies of the blank chart in this chapter and use it to record the results of each heat. I have filled in

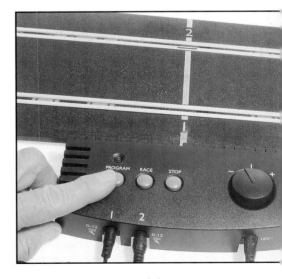

The Scalextric Pacer track has a computer chip that allows you to drive a second car for a few laps and the program will continue to drive that car at the same pace for up to 99 laps. With this accessory, you can actively drive another car on a different lane and "race yourself."

117

one chart with the results of all the heat races to give you an idea of how the chart would look at that period during the race meet. If the lap counter also has a fastest-lap timer, the fastest lap time can be used to brake any ties where two drivers complete the same total number of laps and tenths of a lap.

The Main Event

Let's take a hypothetical example of a race with eight competitors. Jim Jones completed 12.3 laps on the Green Lane, 11.7 on the Yellow Lane, 13.1 on the Blue Lane, and 11.6 on the Red Lane for a race total of 48.7, which was only enough to net him third place. I've totaled the results of the eight Heat Races, but in this example, the Consolation Race No. 1, the Semi-Main Event, and the Main Event are yet to happen.

The drivers with the three-highest numbers of total qualifying laps (D. Blythe, J. Carlson, and B. Battick in this example) will then compete in the Main Event. That leaves one lane open (on this four-lane track) for a fourth driver, and that driver will be the one who wins the Semi-Main Event. The drivers who had the fourth through sixth highest number of Heat Race laps (B. Jones, C. Crank, and J. Jones in this example) qualify for the Semi-Main, with the fourth lane being filled by the driver (either B. Benedict, or S. Arena) who wins the Consolation Race No. 1. If there were more than eight drivers, the ninth-fastest qualifier would race in Consolation Race No. 1, the 10th through 12th would race in Consolation Race No. 2, and the 12th through 14th would race in Consolation Race No. 3. If there are more drivers, you can make a larger chart. The system gives everyone a chance to have at least one bad race and still move up all the way to the Main Event. This is something you'll appreciate when you're the one who had a pickup wire break during your qualifying heat race.

HEATS	Jim Jones	Judy Carlson	Bruce Benedict	Sam Arena	Bill Battick	Carl Crank	Bob Jones	Don Blythe	9	10	11	12	13	14	15	16	17	18
	1	2	3	4	5	6	7	8	9	10	11	12	13	14	15	16	17	18
	12.3	11.8	13.0	11.8														
		11.7	13.1	11.4	12.6													
			11.4	11.7	11.1	11.3												
				12.2	12.4	11.7	11.3											
					12.1	12.4	11.8	11.7										
	11.7					11.8	12.4	13.1										
	13.1	7.3					12.1	12.8										
	11.4	12.2	9.0					12.9										
TOTAL	48.7	49.4	46.4	47.4	48.8	48.1	47.5	50.5										
ORDER	4	2	8	7	3	5	6	1										

CONS. #3		CONS. #2		CONS. #1		SEMI			MAIN		
				Bruce Benedict	Sam Arena	Bob Jones	Carl Crank	Jim Jones	Don Blythe	Judy Carlson	Bill Battick
										PL.	
										PT.	

DATE __October 17__ SCALE EVENT __1/32 Sports__

Here is how the chart might look after four drivers had completed eight heat races (four for each driver, one on each lane of a four-lane track).

Who Is the Champion?

When the next series of races begin, each driver will once again drive for an equal time in each lane, and just as with the Heat Races, the total number of laps and tenths will be entered in each of the four boxes. When all four segments of the Consolation Race No. 1 are complete, B. Benedict and S. Arena will each have a total number of laps, and the one with the highest total moves into the Semi-Main. Again, all four drivers will run an equal amount of time in each of the four lanes, and their laps and tenths of a lap will be totaled to see who won the Semi-Main. The winner of that Semi-Main races in the Main

DATE_____ SCALE _____ EVENT _____

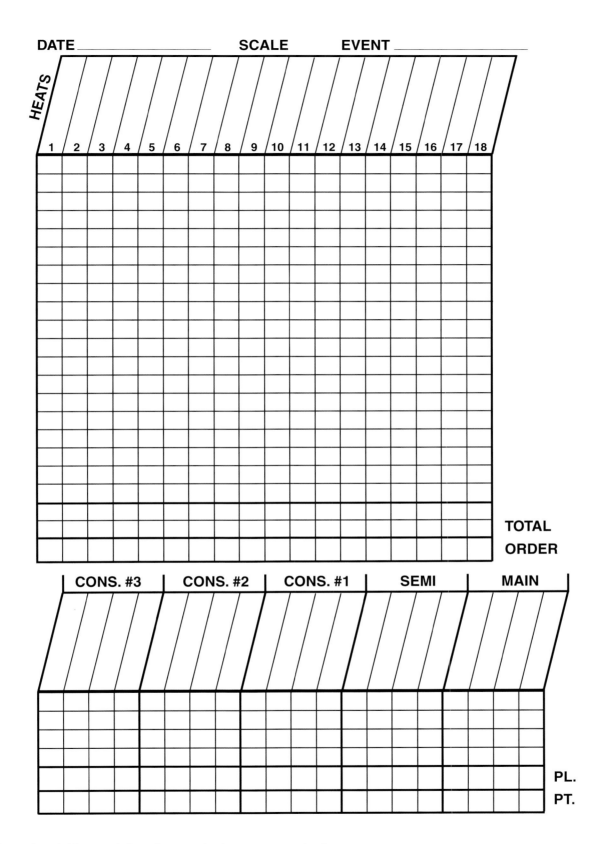

HEATS	1	2	3	4	5	6	7	8	9	10	11	12	13	14	15	16	17	18

TOTAL

ORDER

CONS. #3			CONS. #2			CONS. #1			SEMI			MAIN		

PL.

PT.

Make copies of this record sheet for organized races on your track.

Event. All four drivers race on each lane for an equal time in the Main Event, and their total numbers of laps and tenths of a lap are added to see who won the Main Event. You have the option of making the Consolation Races, Semi-Main, and Main Event run for a longer time than the Heat Races. Usually the Consolation Race and Semi-Main are run for the same times as the Heat Races, and the Main Event may be twice as long or, in some cases, as much as 10 times as long to make it a real challenge of driver skill.

Racing Classes

There are a variety of ways to divide 1/32 scale or HO model cars into different racing classes. The most obvious is to limit the class to cars that have competed in real life. That can be broken into smaller classes by dividing the cars into eras, or by stipulating that only cars that ran in a specific race will constitute a class. The Chart of Racing Classes will give you some examples. I have tried to divide the classes as finely as the available models will allow. Classes can also be combined if you wish. It can be interesting, if not realistic, to watch a Formula One car race against a NASCAR car. After all, model car racing is about fulfilling your own personal racing dreams, and if you delight in watching diverse competition, you can. Classes can be divided further by specifying the country where the cars competed. The Production Sports Cars and the Prototype Sports Cars that competed in the SCCA (Sports Car Club of America) races are considerably different from the cars that have competed at LeMans, the Mille Miglia, at Silverstone, or the Nurburging. There are some specific examples of what cars might fit in each of these classes in chapter 3. Throughout this book you'll also find photos of cars that qualify for these classes.

Vintage Racing

Vintage racing with full-size cars is one of the most popular

Suggested Racing Classes for 1/32-Scale Cars

Production Sports Cars 1930-1949
Production Sports Cars 1950-1960
Production Sports Cars 1961-1970
Production Sports Cars 1975-1985
Production Sports Cars 1985-present
Prototype Sports Cars 1930-1949
Prototype Sports Cars 1950-1960
Prototype Sports Cars 1961-1970
Prototype Sports Cars 1971-1985
Prototype Sports Cars 1984-present
Grand Touring Cars 1930-1949
Grand Touring Cars 1950-1960
Grand Touring Cars 1961-1970
Grand Touring Cars 1971-1985
Grand Touring Cars 1984-present
Formula One Grand Prix Cars 1950-1959
Formula One Grand Prix Cars 1960-1963
Formula One Grand Prix Cars 1962-1970
Formula One Grand Prix Cars 1971-present
Indy, CART & IRL Open-Wheel Cars 1954-1965
Indy, CART & IRL Open-Wheel Cars 1966-present
NASCAR Sedans: 1968-1975
NASCAR Sedans: 1976-present
Trans Am Cars: 1967-1972
Sedans: 1960-1970
Sedans: 1971-present
Rallye Cars: 1996-present
Touring Cars: 1996-present

spectator events in the world of sports and GT cars. With model cars, there are two choices. You can use your own "Time Machine" and re-stage races from the 1950s right down to the proper pit crew and hay bales around the edges of the track. You can also do what the real vintage races do today and combine classes and years into one or more races. At the real races, the cars compete within their own class, just as they do and have always done at LeMans, Sebring, and other sports and GT races.

You Can Have It All

If you love automobiles, electric racing cars (call them slot cars, if you must) may be the best possi-

ble 'vehicle' to satisfy your passion. Only a billionaire can afford to own, maintain, and insure 20 to 100 cars and own the race track to exercise this collection. But you can. And you can change the track to suit your fancy. You have the choices of racing alone, racing against yourself with Scalextric's Pacer, or of racing with your friends. All of this is far more fun than watching a real car race because you are not just imagining that you have the car under control. You are really driving it and watching it being driven at the same time. You even get to pick the cars–and you can pick the moment in racing history you wish to visit to see your collection of automotive art in action.

APPENDIX A: GLOSSARY

Accelerator: See Throttle.

Banked: The term often used to refer to corners that have been tilted or slanted opposite the direction of the car's travel to allow the cars to travel faster through the turn than if it were level.

Borders: Plastic race track pieces that are attached to the outside of the curves or straight to make the track wider. Sliding cars will not hit the guardrails unless they have come out of the slot. These are also called Skid Aprons, Extensions, or Side Tracks.

Brake: Some model car controllers and connector tracks are fitted with a third wire that allows the controller to be used to apply an electric "brake" that is activated when the trigger or push button on the controller is completely released. The electrical circuit turns the motor in the car into a generator to provide what would be called "engine braking" in a real car.

Brake-slide: A driving technique that allows the car to enter a corner at a speed high enough so the car will spin out or leave the slot. Just before the car slides, the throttle is pushed smoothly so the increase in traction "saves" the car and propels it around the corner.

CART (Champion Auto Racing Teams): The real car racing organization that conducts the fastest open-wheeled races in the United States.

Chicane: Special track sections or a series of track sections where the two lanes are moved closer together so the cars can't pass until the chicane widens-out again.

Commercial Track: Slot car racing tracks in stores where you rent time on the track. The tracks are usually routed from chipboard or sheet plastic and have eight lanes. The larger tracks are often as large as 15 x 40 feet and usually race 1/24-scale slot cars with foam rear tires, O-rings for front tires, clear plastic bodies, and only a vague resemblance to any real car. Similar tracks are used by clubs to run HO cars with clear plastic bodies, foam rear tires, and O-ring front tires. The cars in this book are not really intended for use on these large commercial tracks. However, some hobby stores do operate plastic tracks suited to the cars in this book.

Controller: The hand-held device that provides the remote control for the throttle (and optional brake actuation) of a model car. Some controllers are shaped like a pistol with the trigger being used as the throttle, while others are plunger-style where a thumb-operated push-button is used to control the throttle.

Corner Marshals: Race officials who place deslotted cars back into their slots during a race so the drivers can concentrate completely on driving their cars.

Crossing: A single piece of track where the right lane crosses over the left lane through an X-shaped area in the center. Crossings are used in place of figure-8 track arrangements to help equalize the length of the inner and outer lanes. Two crossings are required.

Crossovers: Another term for the overpass bridge used in figure-8 type track designs.

Deslotted: When a car is driven too fast to stay in the slot and spins out, or when the guide shoe is levered from the slot by centrifugal force, the car is said to have been deslotted.

Drafting: A racing maneuver where one car pulls up to within a few inches of the car in front (often referred to as a "tow"). Both cars gain extra speed. The first car breaks the wind, and the car tucked-in behind helps smooth out the airflow over both cars. In a drafting maneuver, both cars can attain higher speeds than either car could alone. Often the second car will pull out from the draft just before the finish line to let the air currents help pull the second car past the first car.

Drift: When a car is running around a corner with the rear wheels and tires tracing a wider arc than the front wheels because the rear wheels and tires are spinning just enough to keep the car in motion. The car is sliding or drifting around the corner, as opposed to simply being powered around the corner without any rear tire slip.

Extensions: See Borders

Figures: Scale model people or animals.

Fishtailing: The action of the car's tail end moving right and left as the car accelerates down the straight. The back-and-forth movement is caused by applying so much throttle that the rear tires are spinning and losing traction.

Foam: The word used to describe model car tires cut from synthetic foam rubber. They are seldom used on the kinds of cars and tracks in this book.

Formula One: The fastest open-wheeled cars in the world. The races are held on tracks all around the world including the

Formula One Grand Prix at Indianapolis, Indiana. The Formula One cars are really the only real cars that are authentic Grand Prix cars, and the races are the only ones that are truly Grand Prix races.

Grid: The formation of racing cars that takes place before the start of the race. The cars line up, on a real track, in the order that they qualified, usually with the car with the fastest qualifying times in the front row placed near the inside of the first corner, the second-fastest qualifier behind that car, and the remaining cars in rows beside the first two cars.

Guide Shoe: The tee-shaped plastic device that pivots beneath the front of the chassis on all the current 1/32-scale cars. The vertical tab on the guide shoe is inserted into the slot on the track to guide the cars around the track. A piece of wire braid is positioned on each side of the tab on the guide shoe. Guide shoes are sometimes called pickup shoes, guide flags, or flags.

Heat Races: Races held to determine which cars will be able to compete in the "Main Event" or final race of the day. The winners (and sometimes the second and third place cars) who "qualify" are allowed to run for the main event.

High Banks: Another term used to define banked turns. The high bank turns generally have a steeper slope than just a banked turn. Because of the steep angle, the upper or outer edge of a banked corner can be several stories off the ground similar to the full-size Daytona International Speedway in Florida.

IRL: Indianapolis Racing League, the organization that stages races for open-wheeled cars at oval and tri-oval tracks throughout America, including the Indianapolis 500 race on Memorial Day.

In-the-Corners Action: My personal term to describe a model race course that is designed to demand the greatest possible level

of skill to negotiate the high-speed corners. It usually applies to a track with at least a few large-radius turns and a minimum amount of tight-radius turns.

Laps: When a race car has been driven once completely around the race track it is said to have completed a single "lap." The duration of some races is determined by a specified number of laps on most model car tracks. On real tracks the race is usually defined either by distance (the Indy 500) or by time (the 24 Hours of Le-Mans). Some of the model car lap counters can be programmed to display the distance or the time in addition to the number of laps.

Marshal: See Corner Marshal.

Nerf: When one car slides-out enough to hit a car on an adjacent lane. The inside car usually has the advantage because it can literally knock the outside car out of its lane.

Oversteer: The term used to describe a car that requires less steering input as the car goes faster through the corner. Usually when a car has oversteer and loses traction, the rear of the car lets go first.

Pickup Shoes: The metal strips on the bottom of an HO car that touch the pickup strips on the track to provide power. Also see guide shoe.

Pickup Strips: The metal strips on the track located on both sides of the slot to provide the carrier to transfer electrical power to the car. The power pack provides the electrical power-feed to the pickup strips through the controller.

Point-and-Shoot: My personal description of what it is like to drive on a model car race track where all of the curves are the same tight radius. This driving technique involves leaving the power on as far into each turn as possible, letting the trigger or push-button on the controller fly off to apply the "brake," and then reapplying as much throttle as quickly as possible to "catch"

the car's slide with powered rear tires before the car has the chance to completely deslot.

Power Pack: The electronic devices that convert conventional household 115-volt AC current into 12 to 18 volts of DC current. The low current makes it unlikely a shock can occur if you touch both pickup strips on the track with one finger. There is enough power that you can feel a tingle.

Powerslide: The term used to describe a driving technique where the car's rear tires are spinning as the car swings through a corner. In most cases, the car will travel faster through the corner with the rear wheels spinning in a powerslide than with the rear tires not breaking traction.

Side Tracks: See Borders.

Silicone Tires: Replacement tires for model racing cars that are molded from silicone rubber rather than the "mechanical" rubber used to mold all the tires on all the cars in this book. Silicone tires can provide a bit more traction on some tracks.

Skid Aprons: See Borders.

Steering: Some model cars have front wheels that are controlled by the action of the pickup or guide shoe (including some MRRC and SCX cars). The steering allows the front wheels to follow the path of the curve even if the rear wheels are sliding out in a much greater arc with the car in a powerslide.

Throttle: The hand controller serves as the accelerator for model cars. You pull a trigger on the pistol-style controls, or push a button on the plunger-style controllers to increase the car's speed. In a real automobile, the floor pedal that controls the throttle and the speed of the car is sometimes called an accelerator pedal.

Understeer: The term used to describe a car that requires more steering input as the car goes faster through the corner. Usually when a car that has understeer loses traction, it is the front of the car that will let go first.

APPENDIX B: SOURCES

Wherever possible, both the mailing address and website for the manufacturer are listed. In some cases, the firm may not have a published mailing address and some firms do not yet have a website. If you contact any of these firms by mail, please have the courtesy to include a stamped, self-addressed envelope if you would like a reply. Many of them charge for their catalogs.

MANUFACTURERS

Airfix Model Kits (also see MRRC)
www.airfix.com/

Any Slot
(See Electric Dreams and other dealers)
1/32 cars, bodies.

Annie Minnie
(See Electric Dreams and other dealers)

Artin
200 Fifth Avenue Building, Room 200
New York, NY 10010
1/32 sets.

Aurora
(See Racemasters)

BSRT
20807 Northeast 8th St.
Redmond, WA 98053
www.scaleauto.com
HO cars, bodies, hop up parts.

Beta & Classic
61 Larkfield Lanes
Southport, Merseyside PR9 8NN
United Kingdom
Cast-resin and clear plastic bodies.

Booth
(see EJ's, Parma, or other dealers)
Clear plastic bodies.

Boye Racing Models
20 W. Cavour St.
Daly City, CA 94014-2229
HO bodies, decals.

Carrera STS Racing GmbH
Sudwest Park 94
Nurnburg 90449,
Germany
www.carrera-toys.de
1/32 cars, track, sets.

Classic
(See Beta)

Cox
(Out of production; see EJ's and Electric Dreams)

Detail Master
P.O. Box 2815
Purceville, VA 20134-2815
detailmaster.com
Etched and cast metal parts 1/24 adaptable to 1/32.

EJ's Hobbies
7017 Cascade Rd. S.E.
Grand Rapids, MI 49546-7304
1/32 cars, parts, bodies, decals

E-R Model Importers
100 So. Main St..
Newark, NY 14513
Distributes Preiser to dealers.

Electric Dreams
3190-H Airport Loop Rd.
Costa Mesa, CA 92680
www.valedtaro.com/elecdrms
Annie Mini, MRE, and Any Slot.

Etzel Speed Classics
P.O. Box 5195
Layfayette, IN 47903-4915
1/32 scale IRL and CART cast-resin bodies

Fly Car Models, S.L.
Ronda de la Buganvilla del Rey
No. 31
Madrid 28023 Spain
www.flycarmodel.com
Cars and parts (see Scalextric USA for America).

Furuli Models
4432 W. Hayward Pl.
Denver, CO 80212
HO cast-resin bodies.

Highway Pioneers models
Dapol Limited
Lower Dec Exhibition Center
Llangoiler, Derbyshire
LL 20 8RX
England
www.dapol.co.uk

Historic Scale Racing Replicas
Box 769
Ukiah, CA 95482
www.p-b-l.com/can-am/
    canamhistorics.html
1/32 scale Can Am cars.

Hot Wheels Racing
(See Mattel)
Diecast and Electric HO cars.

Indy Grips
2034 Woodcrest Rd.
Indianapolis, IN 46227
Silicone tires.

LGB America
6444 Nancy Ridge Drive
San Diego, CA 92121-2296
www.lgb.com
Carrera in North America.

Life-Like
1600 Union Ave.
Baltimore, MD 21211
HO cars and track.

Johnny Lightning
(See Playing Mantis)

MCW Automotive Finishes
Box 518
Burlington, NC 27216-0518
Lacquer paint.

MRRC International Hobbies Ltd.
(See Scalextric USA for America)
P.O. Box 790
St. Heiler JE4 0SW
Jersey, Great Britain
www.mrrc.com
Cars, hop up parts, decals.

MRE
www.mre.co.uk
Decals.

Mattel
333 Continental Blvd.
El Segundo, CA 90245
www.mattel.com/index.asp?f=false
HO and 1/32 -scale cars and track

Mini-Models
7326 Jetty Lane
Houston, TX 77072
www.nu-rora.com
HO cars.

Model Motoring
360 Constance Dr.
Warminster, PA 18974
www.modelmho.com
HO cars, track.

Ninco
(See R.E.H. and Stevens
    International for America)
Ctra. de l'Hospitalet 32
08940 Cornellia
Barcelona, Spain
www.ninco.com
1/32-scale cars, track, parts.

Nostalgia Raceways
(See Mundaring)
1/32-scale cast-resin bodies.

Mundaring Hobby Center
Shop 3, Mundaring Mall,
7025 Great Eastern Highway
Western Australia 6073
Australia
vianet.net.au/~mdghobby/Profile.html
1/32 cast-resin bodies, chassis, parts.

Parma International
13927 Progress Parkway
North Royalton, OH 44133
www.parmapse.com
1/32-scale chassis, hop-up parts, motors, controllers.

Pattos Place
9 Wesley St.
Oatlands
NSW Australia 2117
members.optushome.com.au/
pattosplace/
1/32 clear bodies, decals, wheels.

Pink-Kar
(See Scalextric USA and FL
dealers)
1/32 cars.

Playfit
(See MRRC and dealers)
Motors.

Playing Mantis
3618 Grape Rd.
Mishawaka, IN 46545
playingmantis.com
*Johnny Lightning
Thunderjet 500 HO bodies.*

Pro-Slot
professormotor.com
1/32 cars, motors, decals.

Pro-Track
158 Woodbury St.
Elyria, OH 44035
www.slotcar.org/protrack
1/32 chassis, clear bodies.

R.E.H. Distributors
4415 Marburg Ave.
Cincinnati, OH 45209
*Distributes 1/32 and HO products only
to dealers; your dealer can contact them.*

Racemasters
5544 Vista Del Dia
Anaheim Hills, CA 92807
Imports Tomy A/FX to America.
Racing Champions
(available at larger toy stores)

Revell-Monogram Models
8601 Waukegan Road
Morton Grove, IL 60053
1/32-scale cars.

Riggen
(See R.E.H.)
1/32 track.

SCX
www.scx.es
1/32-scale cars, track, accessories.

Scale Auto
(See BSRT)

Scalextric USA
454 Court C
Tacoma, WA 98402
www.scalextric-usa.com
1/32-scale cars, track, accessories.

Slot Classic
www.telecable.es/personales/slot-
classic
(See Scalextric USA, Monarch
Lines, and other dealers)

Slixx
7411 Garden Grove Blvd., #C
Garden Grove, CA 92841
1/32 decals.

Slot–It
(See Scalextric USA and dealers)
www.slot.it
1/32 motors, magnets, gears, wheels.

Slotech
28 Sandpoint Circle
Ormond Beach, FL 32174-9115
gofastest.com/slottech/
HO hop-up parts, bodies.

Speed Cast Slot Racing Kits
Geocities.com/MotorCity/Speed-
way/2827/

Stevens International
Box 126
Magnolia, NJ 08049
*Distributes 1/32- and HO-scale products
only to dealers, your dealer can contact
them.*

Strombecker
(No longer produced; see R.E.H.
and EJ's Hobbies)
Tomy
(See Racemasters)

Top Slot
IRB Auto Racing
(See Scalextric USA for America)
S.L., Alba, 5
08700 Igualada
Barcelona, Spain
1/32-scale cast-resin bodies.

True Scale Products
www.truescaleproducts.com
1/32- and 1/24-scale clear plastic and resin bodies, wheels and inserts.

Tweaker
(see Scalextric USA)

Tyco
(See Mattel)
Wizard High Performance
148 Deer Oak Lane
Bedford, PA 15522

wizzardho.com
HO hop up parts.

WHERE TO BUY MODEL CAR PRODUCTS

There are thousands of hobby shops that stock 1/32-scale and/or HO-scale products in the United States and worldwide. I have listed dealers that seem to have active websites as this is written. Additional dealers can be found by searching the model car manufacturer's websites. You can locate the nearest dealer by looking in the Yellow Pages under "Hobby and Model Construction Supplies–Retail" or by contacting Scalextric USA, LGB of America for Carrera, and Stevens International or R.E.H. for Ninco. Most hobby dealers carry one or more of these brands.

Cric Crac
Spanish dealer
www.criccrac.com/

Fantasy World Hobbies
7901 Hosmer, Suite A6
Tacoma, WA 98408
www.fantasyworldhobbies.com

Gillett Hobbies
4021 2nd St. N.E.
Columbia Heights, MN 55421
H & T Motor Racing
Bert-Brecht-Str. 43
64291 Darmstadt, Germany
www.ht-motorracing

Monarch Lines
www.monarchlines.co.uk

Mundaring Hobby Center
Shop 3, Mundaring Mall
7025 Great Eastern Highway
Western Australia 6073, Australia
www.vianet.net.au/~mdghobby/Profile.html

NCP
(North Coast Hobbies)
5821 Benton Carrol
Oak Harbor, OH 49449
www.ncphobbies.com

Pattos Place
9 Wesley St.
Oatlands, NSW Australia 2117
www.members.optushome.com.au/pattosplace/

The Race Car Store
28 Milton Ave.
Alpharetta, GA 300004
www.slotcars.net

Rad Trax Slot Car Headquarters
3650 So. Decatur Blvd., #6
Las Vegas, NV 89103
www.radtrax.com/

Scale Auto
www.scaleauto.com/

Slot Car World
Route 1, Box 21
Evant, TX 76525
www.slotcarworld.com

For dealers in the United Kingdom, Spain, Germany Australia and other countires, contact the manufacturer.

WEBSITES WORTH BROWSING

www.modelcarracingmag.com
Model Car Racing magazine, bimonthly, 1/32, HO, and 1/24 slot cars and tracks
www.oldweirdherald.com/
Model Car Racing 'Zine

www.automodelismomagazine.com/
Automodelismo magazine (Spain)

www.scaleautoracing.com
Scale Auto Racing News magazine, bimonthly, mostly commercial, 1/24, 1/32, and HO cars and races

people.goldendome.com/~ken/slotworks.htm
web ring

cygnus.uwa.edu.au/~snowmanf/pages/slotcircuits.html
Tracks of the World in Scalextric

www.scalemodel.net/*site list*

www.zagato.demon.co.uk/scalex
Dave Cheesman

www.circuits-routiers.asso.fr/
French Scalextric

www.partsonly.com/slotlink/index
links

www.mgussin@freeuk.com
Mark Gussin

www.nscc.co.uk
National Scalextric Collectors Club, UK

www.professormotor.com/
Andy Smith

www.slotrace.com
Tracker 2000 track design program

www.slotcargarage.com
Slot Car Garage

www.spies.com/~ahm/ho-slotcars
site list

www.members.home.net/bfergy/
HO plans

www.origin8.com/bradstrack/slotcar
Brad's custom-routed tracks

www.Blueprint69.com/
Automotive blueprints (plans)

www.ukslotcars.co.uk/
catalogof out-of-production
1/32 scale cars

INDEX

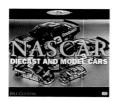

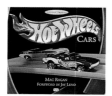
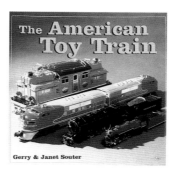

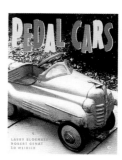